Date Due

MAR 2 1 1995			
	DEC 1 5 2006		
APR 17 '95			
APR 0 1 1996	APR 2 9 2011		
APR 2 2 1996			
MAY 06 1996			
1.4.99			
DEC 1 4 '99			
OCT 2 2 2002			
MAR 0 8 2004			
APR 0 1 2004			
MAY 0 6 2004			
NOV 2 9 2004			
APR 2 0 2005			
DEC 1 2 2005			

Methadone Maintenance in the Management of Opioid Dependence

Methadone Maintenance in the Management of Opioid Dependence

An International Review

Edited by
Awni Arif, M.D., Ph.D.,
and Joseph Westermeyer, M.D., Ph.D.

Foreword by
Norman Sartorius, M.D., Ph.D.

New York
Westport, Connecticut
London

Library of Congress Cataloging-in-Publication Data

Methadone maintenance in the management of opioid dependence : an
   international review / Awni Arif, Joseph Westermeyer [editors].
        p.   cm.
   Includes bibliographical references.
   ISBN 0-275-93392-X (alk. paper)
      1. Methadone maintenance.   2. Opioid habit—Chemotherapy.
   I. Arif, A. E.   II. Westermeyer, Joseph, 1937-   .
   RC568.M4M47   1990
   616.86'32061—dc20   89-78368

Library of Congress Catalog Card Number: 89-78368
ISBN: 0-275-93392-X

First published in 1990

Praeger Publishers, One Madison Avenue, New York, NY 10010
An imprint of Greenwood Publishing Group, Inc.

Printed in the United States of America

∞

The paper used in this book complies with the
Permanent Paper Standard issued by the National
Information Standards Organization (Z39.48-1984).

10 9 8 7 6 5 4 3 2 1

Contents

vi   Contents

Foreword

The World Health Organization, Mental Health Division, is pleased to make this volume available on a topic of increasing international importance and interest. This work has grown out of a WHO collaborative study to which nineteen countries and over thirty experts contributed their time, effort, and support. The stimulus for this collaborative study originated from WHO member countries as well as United Nations agencies concerned with drug dependence problems (such as, the U.N. Fund for Drug Abuse Control and the U.N. Narcotic Control Commission).

This volume is based on papers andpolicy documents received from nineteen member countries. In addition, experts with long experience in this field—clinicians, researchers, program directors—prepared technical papers on program and evaluation at the request of WHO. After collection of these country reports and technical papers, two WHO advisory group meetings were held to critique and review these papers and reports. Following these meetings, the country reports and technical papers were revised. In addition, members of both working groups prepared additional overview, summary, and analysis papers that appear in this volume (see Chapters 5 and 6). In light of the developing AIDS pandemic, and the role of methadone in addressing intravenous drug abuse and unsafe sex practices in drug-dependent persons, Chapters 1 (in part) and 2 (in full) address the critical and current matter of methadone maintenance in the prevention of AIDS.

On behalf of the World Health Organization, I thank the contributors to this volume for their diligent efforts. I also want to express appreciation to the U.N. Fund for Drug Abuse Control for its collaboration and financial assistance in this important endeavor.

Norman Sartorius

Acknowledgments

This volume, developed over five years, represents the combined efforts of over thirty people working in nineteen different countries. Beginning in 1983, reports were invited from those nations known to have considered, studied, or employed methadone in the treatment of opioid addiction. Guidelines for specific information, prepared earlier by us, were supplied to the responsible bureau or ministry. Next, program directors and local experts in methadone maintenance in various parts of the world were asked to prepare reports on the development, policy, and procedures of methadone maintenance on a local level. Experts were asked to prepare reviews on published reports, and some unpublished governmental and programmatic reports.

Two meetings were subsequently held in Minneapolis. The first of these had as its goal to assess, critique, edit, and revise these original papers and reports. In addition to ourselves, the following people participated at this meeting: Dr. James Cooper, National Institute of Drug Abuse, Rockville, U.S.; Dr. James F. Maddux, University of Texas Medical Center, San Antonio, U.S.; Dr. Robert Newman, Beth Israel Medical Center, New York, U.S.; Mr. Jan Ording, World Health Organization, Geneva; Dr. John E. Peachey, Addiction Research Foundation, Toronto, Canada; Dr. Vichai Poshyachinda, Chulalongkorn University Medical Center, Bangkok, Thailand; Dr. Edward Senay, University of Chicago Medical Center, Chicago, U.S.; Dr. Enrico Tempesta, Drug Dependence and Alcoholism Service, Catholic University, Rome,

Italy (observer); Dr. Ambrose Uchtenhagen, Psychiatric University Clinic, Zurich, Switzerland.

Out of this meeting came requests and requirements for additional work revisions, and studies, some of which were in process through 1987. By the end of that year, all country and program reports had been updated and completed. (These reports are being published separately in a monograph at the University of Minnesota. To obtain a copy of this extensive 400-page monograph, please contact the Mental Health Division of the World Health Organization, Geneva, or the Department of Psychiatry and Behavioral Sciences, University of Oklahoma, Oklahoma City.)

The second Minneapolis meeting had the goal of distilling lessons from accumulating studies and reports. Along with Arif and Westermeyer, other participants included the following: Dr. James F. Maddux, University of Texas Medical Center, San Antonio, U.S.; Dr. John F. Peachey, Addiction Research Foundation, Toronto, Canada; Dr. A. H. Tuma, National Institute of Mental Health, Rockville, U.S.; Dr. Ambrose Uchtenhagen, Psychiatric University Clinic, Zurich, Switzerland.

Special acknowledgment is due Ambrose Uchtenhagen for his several contributions to this volume. He has written and/or contributed to several of the chapters. Dr. Uchtenhagen also facilitated the inclusion of European data in this volume, assisting with preparation and translation. He met with us for a final editing of several chapters, following the second Minneapolis meeting. From the inception of the project, down to final preparation for publication, he has been generous in his support and insightful in his counsel.

This work would not have been possible without the financial support and foresight of the U.N. Fund for Drug Abuse Control (UNFDAC). We wish to recognize UNFDAC's key role in underwriting the project.

Other institutions and individuals have provided support in other ways. From the beginning, Dr. Norman Sartorius of the World Health Organization has demonstrated support for and interest in this project. At the University of Minnesota, Dr. Neal Vanselow (Vice-President of Health Sciences) and Dr. Paula Clayton (head of the Psychiatry Department) have provided space, time, and support services during the Minneapolis meetings. Ms. Gloria Wolf saw this volume through its several typings and reorganizations and facilitated scores of international communications. Rachel Westermeyer assisted greatly with meeting arrangements, logistics, and assistance to conference participants. To them also we express our heartfelt appreciation.

Methadone Maintenance in the Management of Opioid Dependence

1

Introduction

Joseph Westermeyer and Awni Arif

Drug dependence involving the opioids has long been internationally recognized as a serious, disabling, and chronic disorder (WHO Committee on Drugs Liable to Produce Addiction 1951). Currently opioid dependence affects millions of individuals and their families, in almost all regions of the world. The Acquired Immunodeficiency Syndrome (AIDS) pandemic has affected an increasing number of intravenous opiate users, exposing not only them but also their sex partners, their unborn children, and other nondrug users who enter the chain of sexual contact with persons infected with the Human Immunodeficiency Virus (HIV). Most countries have had, until recently, few effective medical treatments for use in the rehabilitation of the opioid addict. Problems commonly associated with the disorder have generally been managed by repressive drug laws (Westermeyer 1976). The one exception has been the United Kingdom where, for many years, physicians have been permitted to prescribe heroin to patients abusing illicit opioids (Edwards 1966).

Methadone was synthesized and used in Germany during the Second World War (VanDyke 1949). The short-term medical use of methadone with opioid-dependent patients was first applied in the United States in the 1940s to assist patients' withdrawal from illicit drugs (Vogel, Isbell, and Chapman 1948). Although this methadone-assisted detoxification treatment was effective in reducing or eliminating the withdrawal symptoms on the short term, patients commonly encountered protracted withdrawal sickness and most relapsed to illicit opioid use after the administration of methadone was stopped. In the early 1960s, Vincent Dole and

Marie Nyswander (1965) first prescribed methadone daily over many weeks to assist addicts to reduce illicit drug use and to achieve improved psychosocial functioning. The results of these early studies involving methadone maintenance treatment (MMT) were encouraging and, with relaxation in the legal constraints on doctors to prescribe opioids to addicts, similar programs were started in various cities in the United States and Canada (1963), Sweden (1966), and the Netherlands (1968) (Brill 1973). Unfortunately, the measures developed in these early MMT programs to optimize the methadone use for treatment and to prevent the diversion of methadone into illegal channels were not well developed. Due to widespread over-prescribing and misuse of methadone by physicians, resulting in illicit methadone abuse, amendments to drug legislation governing methadone treatment for addicts were introduced by several governments in the early 1970s. In Canada and the United States these regulations provided guidelines for the use of methadone by the physician in the rehabilitation of addicts, and also included measures to prevent the misuse of methadone and its diversion from licit to illicit channels. Following the early use of methadone in the 1960s in the United States and Canada, methadone was introduced for the treatment of addicts in the United Kingdom (1968), Australia (1970), Hong Kong (1972), France (1973), Italy (1975), and Switzerland (1975).

AN INTERNATIONAL ANALYSIS

The World Health Organization (WHO) has undertaken this study in response to the questions raised by members of the WHO executive board, other country members of WHO, and other United Nations agencies concerned. It includes an analysis of the policies in countries that have had experience in the use of methadone maintenance. (The basis of this analysis is reflected in the nineteen country papers that appear in the monograph published at the University of Minnesota.) One chapter focuses on the impact of AIDS on the policies and practices of methadone prescribing. A summary and recommendations explain the role of methadone in the management of opioid dependence. A chapter on research covers the theoretical and methodological aspects of research on the role of methadone in addiction treatment.

Whereas some countries currently have MMT programs, others have limited or restricted the use of methadone in the treatment of addicts. The availability of methadone for the treatment of addicts varies considerably from country to country. The pattern of methadone use in each country is related to several factors, including the following: (1) sociolegal problems associated with opioid abuse; (2) prevailing professional and public attitudes concerning the management and treatment of the addict; (3) ethical-moral aspects of prescribing an opioid drug such as methadone to addicts; and (4) politicoeconomic aspects of the addiction problem which is often determined by the availability of illicit opioids and the size of the affected patient population. It is not surprising, therefore, that the manner and extent to which methadone is used for the treatment of addicts varies considerably from country to country.   Some countries, such as the Federal Republic of Germany, Austria, and Norway, currently prohibit or limit the use of methadone as a treatment for addicts. Other countries, such as Australia, Canada, and the United States, permit its use but with certain governmental controls and regulations. Still other countries, such as the Netherlands, allow methadone to be used more freely with few guidelines and/or restrictions. In certain countries such as Burma, opium is used rather than methadone. In many countries (for example, Thailand) methadone is prescribed for detoxification of addicts but not for maintenance treatment.

NATIONAL CONSIDERATIONS

The extent and pattern of methadone treatment in many countries is often closely related to the size of the opioid-abusing population. In certain regions of the world, such as the Far East where cultivation of opium occurs, the number of addicts is much greater compared to North America or Europe, where the production and importation of opiates is restricted. On the other hand, the availability of pharmaceutical opioids is greater in certain industrialized countries where there is widespread abuse of such opioids in the addict population. The problems in many countries associated with the abuse of opioid drugs is considerable in financial terms, loss of human resources, or the AIDS risk. Treatment and legal interventions for the management of such problems vary from country to country depending on their financial and treatment resources. Consequently, the role of methadone can be expected to differ throughout the world according to the size and characteristics of the addict population, the types of illicit opioids abused, the nature and availability of resources for the management and control of these problems, and the current phase in the AIDS pandemic. Further compounding these issues in recent years has been a considerable increase in polydrug abuse, particularly among younger patients.

For most countries the primary treatment goal is to achieve a reduction in illicit drug use with the expectation that associated social, psychological, and medical problems will subsequently improve. Despite this common goal, the details of methadone treatment are different from country to country, and from program to program.

THE ROLE OF METHADONE IN TREATMENT

The specific goals for methadone treatment range from the use of methadone for short-term detoxification (detoxification within one month), or long-term detoxification (detoxification within one to six months), and short-term methadone maintenance in which methadone is delivered in a more or less constant dosage from six to twelve months, and long-term methadone maintenance in which methadone is administered in about the same dose for longer than twelve months. Many questions can be asked concerning these treatment strategies. For example, what are the advantages of long-term methadone detoxification over short-term methadone maintenance? Who should receive methadone detoxification and who should receive methadone maintenance? Which of these treatment approaches is most effective for which patients? And can these treatment approaches be used with different patients but at different times within the same treatment system? Because opioid-dependent patients differ considerably from one another, which is the most appropriate treatment duration for each patient? How should drug-free treatment approaches be matched specifically to particular patient characteristics? Which combination of long- or short-term maintenance and long- or short-term detoxification is best for most patients? Some of these questions are addressed in the program reports and country reports in this volume. More research is needed to test the feasibility and effectiveness of each approach.

The coordination of methadone treatment involves many factors besides the administration of methadone. These include its relationship to other forms of treatment, the facilities required for delivering the treatment including inpatient and outpatient facilities, support services, urine-drug testing facilities, and the number and types of treatment staff required. The qualifications for the treatment staff can differ greatly from program to program. The special training of staff has been of particular concern in some countries, especially where inadequate training has been associated with the misuse of methadone.

Additional questions relating to the treatment context involving methadone include such general policies as whether the treatment should be primarily voluntary in nature or should include patients receiving treatment under coercion. In some countries all patients undergoing treatment for opioid dependence are registered with the central authorities; this practice also raises the question of patient confidentiality. Another sensitive area involves policies concerning the assessment of new patients applying for treatment. In some countries, the patients' access to treatment is regulated by legislation. The size of the methadone dose and the duration of treatment may also be regulated by special methadone laws in some countries; these regulations generally reflect the prevailing treatment philosophy in the country concerning the role of methadone in the treatment of opioid addicts. In some countries methadone can be used in high dosages to exert the so-called blockade effect, while in others, only smaller dosages are available to offer symptomatic relief over short periods of time. The question of dosage and duration of treatment is an important consideration for many countries as well as for various programs. In many countries, methadone treatment programs are required to provide psychosocial treatment and other support services. Which treatment modalities should be used together with methadone is a matter of great interest in many countries and is discussed at length in some of the country reports.

The information contained here facilitates an analysis of not only the beneficial aspects of this treatment but also disadvantages which may limit the use of methadone. Data concerning the effectiveness of methadone are found in the form of follow-up studies; these are generally favorable. Despite favorable outcome studies, the relevance of controlled clinical trials of methadone efficacy has been questioned. At this writing, only two careful, randomized placebo-controlled clinical studies of methadone have been carried out. The information contained in the various chapters in the form of country and program reports as well as overview papers should allow readers to form a balanced opinion as to the role of methadone in the treatment of opioid dependence.

The editors would like to emphasize that this volume is based on a wide range of materials, experiences, and observations based on different treatment programs and a broad range of cultural settings in which the programs are imbedded. In most countries the regulations and guidelines are often based on a combination of factors including health economics, and political, historical, ethical and/or religious considerations. Many policies and procedures on methadone treatment are based on clinical experience, others on general psychological and pharmacological principles, and yet others on past medical tradition or customs. A few policies and procedures are based on research evidence from carefully designed and executed studies. Generally, the regulations and guidelines on methadone are based on mixtures of all the previously mentioned sources.

Although this book is dedicated to the role of methadone in the treatment of opioid dependency, we must emphatically point out the critical need for studying other models and approaches to treatment, including other psychopharmacological, psychological, and social approaches. A broad perspective should be taken in planning any treatment program, especially because drug dependency is not the only disabling element among the patient's problems. In most cases drug-dependent persons are suffering from a variety of other psychological, behavioral, and social problems. These include minor and major psychiatric disorders from clinical depression to anxiety, and even to psychosis. Other factors include family loss and conflict, poor premorbid school performance, unemployment, poor social coping, and limited interpersonal skills. The risk to HIV infection and spread intersects with all of these problems and factors. Intervention strategies should contain therapeutic elements to address these various factors in addition to the problem of drug use. A comprehensive approach is critical in the development of any intervention strategies, taking into consideration the existing mental health services and the primary health care system, with the possibility of integration of the drug dependence program into these services.

AIDS AND METHADONE TREATMENT

The Acquired Immunodeficiency Syndrome is caused by the Human Immunodeficiency Virus, a retrovirus. AIDS is an illness for which no cure is available at this time. First described in 1981, transmission has been shown to occur through blood transfusion, blood products (such as gamma globulin), injections, pregnancy (from mother to fetus), tattoos and skin piercing, organ and semen donation, and certain medical procedures, for example, contamination while drawing blood (Mann 1987; Weiss et al. 1985). Sexual intercourse (both heterosexual and homosexual) and transplacental transmission to the unborn fetus are major causes of the HIV pandemic in some regions (Winkelstein et al. 1987; Redfield et al. 1985; Quinn et al. 1986). Exposure to HIV among opioid drug-dependent persons is a primary cause in many areas (Drucker 1986; Tidone, Goglio, and Borra 1987).

Prevention of HIV among opioid and other drug-dependent persons presents special problems. Special educational techniques and strategies must be employed, because many such persons are not accessible through the usual mass media and other social channels. Even if exposed to such education and accepting of it, intoxication or withdrawal states can affect their earlier resolve. One tactic has been to provide intravenous drug users with sterile needles; this approach has many of the same ethical and political dilemmas of methadone; for example, does providing needles indicate official approval of drug use? (Francis and Chin 1987). Even with clean needles, intoxicated drug users can make decisions which expose them to HIV risk through a casual sex partner or less safe sexual practices. Methadone maintenance has been suggested as a potentially valuable tool in reducing HIV through several means, as follows: (1) eliminating the intravenous route of drug administration; (2) reducing or eliminating periods of intoxication and withdrawal, which can lead to unsafe sexual practices; and (3) fostering psychosocial recovery from drug dependence so that casual sex partners, prostitution, and less safe sex practices are unlikely to occur. So far, the efficacy of methadone maintenance in reducing the rate of HIV in persons-at-risk has not been demonstrated through careful research. At the time of this writing, however, such projects are being planned. Of interest, Tidone et al. in Italy (Tidone, Goglio, and Borra 1987) observed HIV seropositivity in only 28 percent of methadone maintenance patients as compared to 41-53 per cent HIV seropositivity in three other addict groups (including those in a therapeutic community) (Tidone, Goglio, and Borra 1987).

REFERENCES

Brill L. International maintenance programs, in CD Chambers and L Brill (eds.), *Methadone Experiences and Issues*, 325-346. New York: Behavioral Publications, 1973.

Dole VP and Nyswander ME. A medical treatment of diacetylmorphine (heroin) addiction, *J. Amer. Med. Assoc.* 193:646-650, 1965.

Drucker E. AIDS and addiction in New York City, *Amer. J. Drug Alcohol Abuse* 12:165-181, 1986.

Edwards G. The British approach to the treatment of heroin addicts, *Yale Law Review* 78:1175, 1966.

Francis D and Chin J. The prevention of Acquired Immunodeficiency Syndrome in the United States, *J. Amer. Med. Assoc.* 257:1357-1360, 1987.

Mann J. AIDS, *World Health Forum* 8:361-370, 1987.

Quinn TC et al. AIDS in Africa: An epidemiologic paradigm, *Science* 234:955-963, 1986.

Redfield RR et al. Heterosexually acquired HTLV-III/LAV disease (AIDS related complex and AIDS), *J. Amer. Med. Assoc.* 254:2094-2096, 1985.

Tidone L, Goglio A, and Borra GC. AIDS in Italy (letter), *Amer. J. Drug Alcohol Abuse* 13:485-486, 1987.

VanDyke HB. New analgesic drugs, *Bull. New York Acad. Sciences* 25:152-175, 1949.

Vogel VH, Isbell H and Chapman KW. Present status of narcotic addiction, *J. Amer. Med. Assoc.* 138:1019-1026, 1948.

Weiss SH et al. HTLV-III infection among health care workers; Association with needle-stick injuries, *J. Amer. Med. Assoc.* 254:2089-2093, 1985.

Westermeyer J. The pro-heroin effects of anti-opium laws, *Arch. Gen. Psychiatry* 33:1135-1139, 1976.

Winkelstein W et al. Sexual practices and risk of infection by the human immunodeficiency virus, *J. Amer. Med. Assoc.* 257:321-352, 1987.

World Health Organization Committee on Drugs Liable to Produce Addiction: Third Report. WHO Technical Report 57. Geneva: WHO, 1951.

2

Impact of AIDS Epidemiology on Methadone Policy

Ambrose Uchtenhagen

During the last years, HIV infection and AIDS disease among intravenous drug users have increased in absolute figures and in relation to other high-risk groups. In Europe, I.V. drug users (IVDU) composed only 5 percent of 48 AIDS cases registered in 1985, whereas in 1988 IVDU were 25.2 percent of 4,804 cases (figures from WHO Collaborating Centre on AIDS, Paris). The risk group of IVDU shows the highest increase rates as compared to homosexuals.

The AIDS risk has led to a reconsideration of national drug policy strategies and priorities in Europe and North America. Preventive measures (preventing AIDS infection among I.V. drug users and preventing I.V. drug use per se) have become more critical. Other alternatives have included the availability of syringes, promulgation of safe sex practices, and reconsideration of methadone policy in various places. In countries such as the Federal Republic of Germany and Austria, where methadone maintenance has not been permitted, pilot experiments on this approach have been carried out. Other countries, for example, the Netherlands and Italy, have tried to attract a maximum number of I.V. drug users to methadone maintenance (Hummel et al. 1986). Steps to propagate methadone maintenance have been as follows:

- sufficient funding for additional methadone programs;
- lowering the threshold for entering methadone maintenance programs (no age limit, no previous attempts for drug-free treatment);

- relaxing the expectations and regulations on reducing concomitant illegal drug use, on life-style changes and on psychosocial treatment.

This policy and these procedures need careful evaluation. To what extent can the spread of AIDS infections be realistically contained by methadone maintenance? What is the evidence? Is it possible to reduce the annual number of new infections by expanding methadone programs or by changing methadone regulations? Is this expectation of methadone in controlling AIDS comparable to former expectations; that is, that methadone would eliminate the illegal heroin market or that methadone would reduce dependence-related delinquency?

A realistic assessment has to consider issues such as the following:

- identification of behavioral changes relevant for diminishing the risks of AIDS infection;
- adequate strategies to facilitate these behavioral changes;
- contribution of methadone maintenance to the intended behavioral changes;
- predictors for the intended behavioral changes through methadone maintenance.

BEHAVIORAL CHANGES FOR DIMINISHING RISKS OF AIDS INFECTION

AIDS infection is disseminated among I.V. drug users by needle sharing and by sexual transmission (Harms et al. 1987; Battjes and Pickens 1988). The first mode of transmission affects the drug-using community exclusively, whereas the second mode concerns all sexual partners (including nondrug users) of contaminated persons. Behavioral changes must, therefore, be sought with respect to both needle sharing and unsafe sex.

The chain of infection caused by needle sharing can be broken by either abstinence from injecting drugs or by limiting needles and syringes to strictly personal use (Hopkins 1988; Tempesta and DiGiannantonio 1988; Des Jarlais et al. 1988). Prerequisites for refraining from needle sharing in the target population are as follows: (1) adequate information; (2) motivation; (3) availability of needles and syringes. Use of bleach in disinfecting used syringes may be considered a substitute for the latter in a milieu with restricted availability of needles and syringes (Newmeyer 1988).

Regarding the transmission of AIDS infection through sexual contact, the use of condoms alone is an adequate measure for breaking the chain of infection. Sexual abstinence is another alternative. Prerequisites are again adequate information and motivation of those concerned, especially sexual partners of potentially contaminated persons. This includes the clients of contaminated prostitutes. Adequate availability of condoms is also important.

A third mode of transmission with growing importance is childbirth by contaminated mothers. Children of these mothers stay seropositive at a 40 to 60 percent rate. Because abortion in contaminated women is often refused or missed, adequate prevention requires the foregoing measures, especially the use of condoms as a contraceptive and as a protective device.

STRATEGIES FOR PREVENTIVE BEHAVIORAL CHANGE

Few studies have been made on the effectiveness of various strategies in affecting behavioral changes. Information disseminated solely by pamphlets is disappointingly inefficient, as shown in a German pilot study (Arnold and Frietsch 1987).

A U.S. pilot study demonstrated a high degree of relevant information among I.V. drug users on transmission of AIDS-infection, AIDS-symptoms, and ways of risk reduction, but also a substantial deficit in self-organization. By comparison, homosexual groups were much more effective in producing widespread behavioral change (Friedman et al. 1987).

A first study from London drug dependence clinics evaluated the effects of free availability of syringes among their clients. Thirty percent of clients changed their behavior and switched to using new syringes for each injection (Stimson and Oppenheimer 1982). D. Des Jarlais et al. (1985) reported similar observations from the United States. Even better results were published by British colleagues lately (Ghodse et al. 1987; Robertson et al. 1988; Strang et al. 1987). However, the overall impact of the approach should not be overestimated. In Italy syringes were largely available at an early stage, but AIDS-infection among I.V. drug users is comparatively high. This example indicates the preventive limits of this approach as an isolated measure (WHO report 1987). Exchange and even free availability of syringes and needles alone is unable to produce major behavioral change, as demonstrated in an unpublished pilot study in Zurich. Especially the younger I.V. drug users who are not yet contaminated responded to available needles and syringes in extremely low numbers. Among 313 subjects studied, the vast majority of all involved drug users obtained free syringes and needles only sporadically.

In contrast, drug users in a stable therapeutic relationship have shown a high affinity to improve their risk-taking behavior. In a study on ninety-seven outpatient drug users in Zurich, subjects who underwent AIDS-antibody testing showed a significantly higher compliance in comparison to those who refused testing. No major differences in compliance were found between test-positive and test-negative subjects (Haas and Kurz 1988). In other studies, a maximum of risk-taking reduction was found in seropositive subjects (Robertson et al. 1988). The first step to behavioral change, therefore, is the willingness to take the test and to work through the corresponding information, and the implications of a negative or positive test result. This process—including adequate hygiene in the use of injection materials, use of condoms for safer sex, compliance in medical and psychological treatment—can be achieved within a therapeutic relationship over at least a few months' duration (Haas and Kurz 1988).

Similar observations concern the issue of safer sex among drug users. Offering condoms alone is not adequately effective because the use of condoms is not easily accepted. An important risk group is female partners of male drug users who refrain from using condoms for a variety of reasons (Des Jarlais et al. 1985). This risk is lowered if a therapeutic relationship is established. Fears can then be identified, such as being an AIDS-contaminated person or losing one's partner. Once identified, these fears can be ameliorated (Mondanaro 1987).

CONTRIBUTION OF METHADONE MAINTENANCE TO PREVENTIVE BEHAVIORAL CHANGES

To what extent does methadone maintenance facilitate stable therapeutic relationships for outpatient I.V. drug users? Observations differ from place to place, and from program to program. Nevertheless, stabilization over months and years is better documented for patients in methadone maintenance programs than for patients in drug-free ambulatory treatment (Sells et al. 1976). Methadone maintenance can contribute to the establishment of therapeutic relationships that facilitate responsible behavior and reduction of risk-taking behavior. In a Zurich study, the intended behavioral change is significantly higher in methadone maintenance patients as compared to patients in drug-free ambulatory treatment (Haas and Kurz 1988). Yet, no conclusive replication studies demonstrate this in a satisfying manner with adequate statistics.

To what extent is methadone maintenance able to attract and to keep in treatment drug users who would otherwise be exposed to the risks of the street or prison milieu? Such estimations are not easy to make, and the relevant factors probably vary from place to place. Where the total number of methadone patients exceeds the total number of drug users in all other forms of treatment (whether due to unequal distribution of resources, treatment slots, or other reasons), it would be hard to deny that methadone maintenance plays an active role in risk reduction.

Direct proof for a protective function of methadone treatment is difficult to demonstrate. A number of complex variables are operating, and a foolproof experimental design is not feasible. Reduction of I.V. drug use and of needle sharing has been demonstrated repeatedly, for example, in a three-year field study of methadone maintenance programs in New York City, Philadelphia, and Baltimore, with a total of 388 patients involved (Ball et al. 1988). A U.S. study by D. M. Novick et al. (1986) compared infection rates over time, demonstrating a significantly lower rate among those engaged in a methadone maintenance program as compared to other I.V. drug users. A similar trend has been demonstrated in a Swiss study which documented zero seroconversion in a sample of 21 seronegative methadone patients over 34 months; no patients in this well-structured program acquired an HIV infection although almost half of them did not completely abstain from IVDU (Huber-Stemich and Haas 1989). However, there is as yet no proven relationship between availability and extent of methadone maintenance on one hand, and overall rates of AIDS infection among drug users in a given region or country on the other hand.

PREDICTORS FOR PREVENTIVE BEHAVIORAL CHANGE

Similar scientific evidence exists on this issue so far. Small-scale studies and everyday practice suggest, however, that predictors for behavioral change are almost identical with predictors for successful methadone maintenance, as measured on various behavioral levels. These latter include developing a productive life-style, refraining from delinquency and illegal drug use, and maintaining satisfying social contacts and leisure activities. Outcome predictors are mainly the quality of therapeutic relationship and compliance with treatment requirements (Erlanger, Haas, and Baumann 1987). J. Ball et al. (1988) found a correlation between positive outcome, length of stay, and quality of treatment. One may expect, therefore, that methadone maintenance without establishing a stable therapeutic relationship and without the usual treatment requirements (such as controlled intake of noninjectible methadone and urinalyses) will be less effective in obtaining the intended behavioral changes concerning injection hygiene and sexual contacts. Controlled evidence, however, is not available at this time.

ADDITIONAL RISKS FOR METHADONE MAINTENANCE PATIENTS

Eventual side effects of methadone maintenance on the immune system must be considered. Any stressor on the immune system increases the risk for its breakdown, with subsequent manifestation of AIDS disease in a contaminated person. If methadone maintenance is a stressor, illegal street drugs are even more so. Certainly, drug abstinence would be preferable, including abstinence from methadone, whenever attainable. On the other hand, we do not have evidence for any facilitating role of methadone maintenance in reducing an eventual resistance to HIV infection. Rates of seropositivity in patients on methadone maintenance reflect rather the duration of their drug career and, therefore, the duration of exposure to AIDS infection, more than anything else. The effects of methadone maintenance on the risk for ensuing HIV infection or manifest AIDS disease are not yet sufficiently documented.

SUMMARY AND CONCLUSIONS

The present state of knowledge does not allow us to draw definitive conclusions. Some observations and findings, however, indicate that behavioral changes effective in reducing the risk for AIDS transmission are facilitated in therapeutic programs utilizing methadone maintenance. However, it is necessary to provide other treatment to produce a life-style change. Certain treatment regulations and an adequate therapeutic relationship must be available along with methadone.

Reduction of risk for HIV transmission (and reinfection) is achieved in numerous individual cases. Other intended behavioral changes (for example, productivity and recreation) are also necessary.

An impact of any one treatment modality on AIDS epidemiology at large is rather unlikely. This includes the modality of methadone maintenance, which has already failed in eliminating the active illegal drug market and the extent of drug-related delinquency. This ineffectiveness is due to limited attractiveness of treatment programs for drug-dependent persons. Expanding methadone maintenance and its attractiveness by reducing the relevant requirements and by asking for less compliance with regulations will probably be ineffective in obtaining the intended changes in risk-taking behavior.

AIDS epidemiology will have little influence on the structure and requirements of effective methadone maintenance programs. However, AIDS epidemiology will affect the medical, psychological, and psychosocial needs of patients engaged in drug treatment programs, and probably the number of patients applying for methadone maintenance.

REFERENCES

Arnold T and Frietsch R. Zur AIDS-Prolematik in der Drogenarbeit: Ergebnisse einer Klientenbegragung, *Suchtgefahren* 233:237–248, 1987.

Ball JC, et al. Reducing the risk of AIDS through methadone maintenance treatment, *J. Health Soc. Behav.* 29:214–226, 1988.

Battjes RJ and Pickens WR (eds.). *Needle Sharing among Intravenous Drug Abusers: National and International Perspectives*, NIDA Research Monograph 80, DHHS publication number (ADM) 88–1567, 1988.

Buning ED, van Brussel GHA, and van Senten G. Amsterdam's drug policy and its implications for controlling needle sharing, in Battjes RJ and Pickens RW (eds.), *Needle Sharing among Intravenous Drug Abusers: National and International Perspectives*, NIDA Research Monograph 80, DHHS publication number (ADM) 88–1567, 59–74, 1988.

Cooper JR et al. (eds.). *Research on the Treatment of Narcotic Addiction: State of the Art*, NIDA Treatment Research Monograph Series, DHHS publication number (ADM) 83–1281, 1983.

Des Jarlais DC, Friedman SR, and Hopkins W. Risk reduction for the Acquired Immunodeficiency Syndrome among intravenous drug users, *Ann. Intern. Med.* 103: 755–759, 1985.

Des Jarlais DC et al. The sharing of drug injection equipment and the AIDS epidemic in New York City: The first decade, in Battjes RJ and Pickens RW (eds.), *Needle sharing among Intravenous Drug Abusers: National and International Perspectives,* NIDA Research Monograph 80, DHHS publication number (ADM) 88–1567, 160–175, 1988.

Erlanger A, Haas H and Baumann I. Therapieerfolg von Methadonnpatienten mit unterschiedlicher Indikation, *Drogalkohol* 11:3–15, 1987.

Friedman SR et al. AIDS and self-organization among intravenous drug users, *Int. J. Addict.* 22(3):201–219, 1987.

Ghodse AH, Tregenza G, and Li M. Effect of fear of AIDS on sharing of injection equipment among drug abusers, *Brit. Med. J.* 295:698–699, 1987.

Haas H and Kurz T. Psychische auswirkungen des HIV-Tests bei drogenabhangigen, *Schweiz Rundschau Med (PRAXIS)* 77/21:582–586, 1988.

Harms G et al. Risk factors for HIV infection in German I.V. drug users, *Klin. Wochenschr.* 65:376–379, 1987.

Hopkins W. Needle sharing and street behavior in response to AIDS in New York City, in Battjes RJ and Pickens RW (eds.) *Needle Sharing among Intravenous Drug Abusers: National and International Perspectives,* NIDA Research Monograph 80, DHHS publication number (ADM) 88–1567, 1988.

Huber-Stemich F and Haas H. Pravention der HIV-infektion im methadonprogramm, *Sozialpsychiatrischer Dienst der Psychiatrischen Universitatsklinik Zurich (zur Publikation vorgesehen,* 1989.

Hummel RF et al. (eds.). *AIDS Impact on Public Policy.* New York: Plenum Press, 1986.

Mondanaro J. Strategies for AIDS-prevention: Motivation health behavior in drug-dependent women, *J. of Psychoactive Drugs* 19(2):143–150, 1987.

Newmeyer JA. Why bleach? Development of a strategy to combat HIV contagion among San Francisco intravenous drug users, in Battjes RJ and Pickens RW (eds.), *Needle Sharing among Intravenous Drug Abusers: National and International Perspectives,* NIDA Research Monograph 80, DHHS publication number (ADM) 88–1567, 151–159, 1988.

Novick DM, et al. Abstract of clinical research findings: Therapeutic and historical aspects in Harris LS (ed.), *Problems of Drug Dependence (1985)*, NIDA   Research Monograph Series 67, 318–320, 1986.

Power RM. The influence of AIDS upon patterns of intravenous use: Syringe and needle sharing among illicit drug users in Britain, in Battjes RJ and Pickens RW (eds.), *Needle Sharing among Intravenous Drug Abusers: National and International Perspectives*, NIDA Research Monograph 80, DHHS publication number (ADM) 88–1567, 75–88, 1988.

Robertson JR, Skidmore CA, and Roberts JJK. HIV infection in intravenous drug users: A follow-up study indicating changes in risk-taking behaviour, *Brit. J. Addict.* 83:387–391, 1988.

Sells SB, et al. A national follow-up study to evaluate the effectiveness of drug abuse treatment: A report on the DARP five years later, *Am. J. Drug Alcohol Abuse* 4:545–556, 1976.

Stimson G and Oppenheimer E. *Heroin Addiction.* London: Tavistock, 1982.

Strang J, Heathcote S, and Watson P. Habit-moderation in injecting drug addicts, *Health Trends* 19:16–18, 1987.

Tempesta E, and Di Giannantonio M. Sharing needles and the spread of HIV in Italy's addict population, in Battjes RJ and Pickens RW (eds.), *Needle Sharing among Intravenous Drug Abusers: National and International Perspectives*, NIDA Research Monograph 80, DHHS publication number (ADM) 88–1567, 100–113, 1988.

World Health Organization. AIDS Among Drug Abusers, Report on WHO Consultation Stockholm, October 1986. Geneva: WHO, 1987.

3

Methadone in the Treatment of Opioid Dependence: A Review of the World Literature

Edward C. Senay and Ambrose Uchtenhagen

The concept of using legal opioids in the treatment of opioid dependence dates back at least one hundred years. In the nineteenth century, the King of Siam decreed that opium should be dispensed by the state to opium-dependent persons. At the turn of the century, the Spanish dispensed legal opioids to indigenous Chinese in the Philippines, a practice that was not continued after the United States took control of the Philippines in the Spanish-American War (Musto 1973). The system was terminated not because of its cost and benefits but because legal provision of opioids was ideologically repugnant to policymakers in the United States. In the early 1920s the use of morphine in American maintenance clinics was terminated when courts ruled that physicians could not use opioids to maintain opioid dependence. In England, the Rolleston Commission in 1924 ruled that English physicians could dispense heroin and morphine to treat opioid dependence if they saw fit. The English changed this policy in 1967 to limit the use of opioids in the treatment of opioid-dependent persons to specially licensed practitioners, because poor prescribing procedures had led to epidemics of heroin dependence (May 1973).

Methadone was synthesized during World War II by the German pharmaceutical company Hoechst, to replace opiate analgesics, in a period of insufficient supply. Its use in the treatment of opiate dependence was first restricted to detoxification purposes. Methadone maintenance as a treatment modality was closely associated in time with a marked rise in the prevalence and incidence of heroin dependence.

In the 1950s, a Joint Commission of the New York State Medical Society and the American Bar Association called for an evaluation of legal opioid substitution for heroin addicts. This action paved the way for the work of Vincent Dole and Marie Nyswander at Rockefeller University in New York City in the mid-1960s. In their original work, patients were admitted to a hospital for a period of weeks. During this time methadone was given daily and the dose increased to the point at which most street doses of heroin would have no effect. This is referred to as blockade of other opioid effects. Patients were then discharged to the community and attended outpatient clinics. Dole and Nyswander found that about 80 percent of unreachable heroin addicts were markedly improved by methadone maintenance therapy (Dole and Nyswander 1965; Dole and Nyswander 1968).

Success rates have not continued to be as high as those reported initially by Dole and Nyswander. They excluded complicated clinical cases from their early studies, although such difficult cases were treated when methadone became standardized and in widespread use. In the past twenty years, methadone has been used in varied social, economic, and cultural settings. Several countries have acquired over two decades of experience with the therapeutic use of methadone, both for maintenance and in withdrawal in opioid-dependent persons. Australia, Austria, Burma, Canada, Denmark, France, Hong Kong, Italy, the Netherlands, Pakistan, Spain, Sweden, Switzerland, Thailand, the United Kingdom, and the United States have permitted the use of methadone in the treatment of opioid addiction under certain conditions.

The effectiveness of methadone maintenance, per se, is difficult to discuss because it is usually used in the context of a broader treatment effort in which psychological and medical care, referral for vocational and educational counseling, legal assistance, family therapy, and other services are included. Any discussion of methadone on an international basis is also difficult because treatment models differ from country to country. For example, in Europe and Asia methadone tends to be used within traditional medical or social facilities by professionals, such as physicians, social workers, and psychologists. On the contrary, in the United States methadone programs tend to be staffed largely by former addicts.

In a number of European countries, the public and professional debate on methadone maintenance programs is still controversial. The Acquired Immunodeficiency Syndrome epidemic has contributed to this dialogue in recent years. Publications on the pros and cons of methadone maintenance as a strategy against AIDS are not considered in this review. The focus here is restricted to evaluation studies, clinical studies and various regulations concerning methadone maintenance in Europe.

PHARMACOLOGY OF MEDICINE

Methadone, first synthesized in Germany in the 1940s, is d,1-4, 4-diphenyl-6-dimethyl-amino-3-heptanone. The 1 isomer accounts for most of its activity. Methadone has effects similar to those of morphine. Single doses of either drug in a naive subject produce analgesia, sedation, respiratory depression, and in some subjects, euphoria. Five to 10 mg. of methadone give analgesia which is comparable in intensity and time course to 10 to 15 mg. of morphine (Jaffe and Martin 1975; Kreek 1979).

When taken orally in sufficient dosage, methadone suppresses the opioid withdrawal syndrome for 12 to 24 hours or longer, much longer than can be achieved with morphine. Daylong suppression of the abstinence syndrome and oral effectiveness make methadone useful in maintenance programs because no other opioid has these two characteristics.

Methadone depresses the respiratory center, has antitussive action, and produces mild hyperglycemia and hypothermia. Methadone inhibits gastrointestinal tone and propulsive activity and can cause biliary tract spasm, but does not have major effects on the pregnant uterus. Tolerance to the miotic effects of methadone develops rapidly. Methadone is well absorbed from the stomach in most individuals, and large concentrations appear in the plasma within minutes after oral administration. The drug enters tissues throughout the body with only a small amount traversing the blood-brain barrier. Methadone appears to be bound to tissue protein. Biotransformation in the liver is probably through N-demethylation and cyclization to form pyrrolidines. The half-life of methadone in nontolerant individuals is about fifteen hours.

When used as an analgesic in routine practice, delirium, hallucinations, and hemorrhagic urticaria rarely have been reported. There are no reports of such effects in methadone maintenance patients.

Recent research indicates that with chronic administration, pools of methadone accumulate in body tissues. Methadone from these pools provides a fairly constant blood concentration. Like other opioids, methadone crosses the placental barrier, and chronic administration in a pregnant mother results in a methadone-dependent neonate. Withdrawal from all opioids in neonates, methadone included, seems to be more variable in its expressions, more delayed in its onset, and more extended in time in comparison to adult withdrawal.

During the early phases of methadone treatment, several biochemical and physiological abnormalities have been observed (Kreek 1979). For example, there is a decrease in plasma levels of reproduction related peptide hormones, such as follicle stimulating hormone (FSH) and luteinizing hormone (LH). All of these abnormalities appear to return to normal after two to ten months of treatment. Thyroid abnormalities and persistence of protein and immunologic abnormalities have been observed, but these probably reflect years of use of unsterile needles and solutions. Theodore Cicero et al. found that methadone maintenance patients have decreased ejaculate volume and decreased sperm counts (Cicero et al. 1975). The time course and clinical significance of these findings is not known.

Overdose of methadone can be treated with naloxone, but naloxone may have to be repeated because its effects last only two hours while methadone effects can last much longer (Kjeldgaard et al. 1971; Waldron, Klint, and Seibel 1973). Methadone overdose cases need to be observed closely for twenty-four to forty-eight hours, preferably in a hospital.

Methadone maintenance appears to be medically safe (Kleber, Stobetz, and Mezritz 1980). Common side effects are as follows: sedation, if the dose is too high; constipation, which can be treated by increasing fluid intake and using stool softeners; sweating; occasional transient ankle edema in females; and changes in libido. These changes are usually ameliorated by dose reduction. All the side effects just cited improve with time alone. Rarely, patients complain of skin problems (such as pruritus), but these also improve with time or with symptomatic treatment. Daily administration of opioids increases the possibility of synergism with other psychoactive drugs. Patients in many U.S. clinics must take breathalyzer tests before methadone is administered. If blood alcohol concentrations are 0.05 Gm. percent or above, patients are not given methadone on that day until blood alcohol concentrations are under 0.05 Gm. percent. Users of multiple drugs who are on methadone are at risk for lethal effects from synergism if they continue multiple drug use.

Studies of the biotransformation of methadone indicate wide interindividual variability in blood levels following identical dosing regimens. This research suggests that poor responders to treatment may not absorb methadone from the gastrointestinal tract normally (Kelly, Welch, and McKnelley 1978). Liver and renal disease may account for some of the individual variation.

A number of investigators have found that methadone does not appear to interfere with reaction time (Gritz et al. 1975). Methadone-maintained patients do not appear to have memory deficits, but chronic administration of methadone was found to differentiate performance of patients from controls on recall. Clinically these effects are not noticeable. A study of driving records contained no evidence to restrict driving privileges of methadone maintenance patients (Maddux, Williams, and Ziegler 1977). Methadone maintenance clinics have patients representing many occupations in modern urban centers.

CLINICAL ASPECTS OF METHADONE MAINTENANCE TREATMENT

The immediate clinical goal of maintenance therapy is to provide a dose of methadone that suppresses opioid abstinence symptoms for the entire twenty-four hour period between doses without producing euphoria, sedation, or dulling of consciousness (Senay 1983; Wieland and Chambers 1970). This dose relieves the addict of major sources of pressure to use illicit opioids; namely, the dysphoria of opioid abstinence. Changes are made in the dose if clinically undesirable effects occur. Many patients do not want to be sedated or euphoric because they want to have their minds clear to work on their problems. Some patients may seek euphoria or sedation, but these need not occur if dose effects are medically monitored. A dose of methadone that relieves abstinence dysphoria also relieves the addict of the pressure to get drugs to feel normal. Studies indicate that during treatment, rates of crime go down substantially (McGlothlin 1979).

Another goal of methadone maintenance is to engage the addict in a therapeutic relationship both with a counselor and with a program. *Therapeutic* is broadly defined here to include social, vocational, legal, or other services in addition to psychological help. In many methadone programs in the United States counselors are utilized who have been addicts themselves and have been treated successfully. They provide what might be called affiliative counseling because they personify the transition between addiction and abstinence from illicit drugs.

The stereotype of an addict in treatment is one of a manipulative person who has no interest in changing from a life-style centered on intoxication. There are addicts who fit the stereotype but to characterize all addicts by this stereotype belies the data and dehumanizes them. Addicts are often intensely ambivalent about their drug habits and deviant life-styles. Many make repeated attempts to change. Therapy depends on building successful links with the healthy pole of the ambivalence. When addicts try to manipulate staff for antitherapeutic ends, they should be confronted.

In addition to eliminating abstinence dysphoria, freeing patients from the need to engage in criminal behavior, and providing a therapeutic relationship, maintenance therapy aims to improve the health status of addicts. On admission to treatment, addicts commonly have a number of health problems. Minor problems, such as abscesses, phlebitis, and dental caries, can be treated successfully. Major problems such as hepatitis, endocarditis, and susceptibility to major infections (pneumonia, malaria, tuberculosis and lately Acquired Immunodeficiency Syndrome) need to be identified and referred for therapy. The health status of maintenance patients tends to improve during treatment (Christakis et al. 1973; Finnegan 1979 a and b; Longwell et al. 1979). Patients usually gain weight. Women usually experience a return of normal menstrual cycles (Finnegan 1979). During runs of heroin use many female addicts develop menstrual abnormalities; they appear to be more likely to become pregnant during treatment probably because there is an improvement in nutrition and because legal opioids provide relative freedom from the stress of a criminal life-style.

Dole theorized that methadone would block the reinforcing effects of heroin. Without reinforcement, the conditioned response involved in repeated use of heroin would become weak and disappear. Vincent Dole recommended high doses of methadone, in the order of 80 to 120 mg. a day or more, so that addicts could not use enough heroin to achieve euphoria. The issue of dose and outcome efficacy is not resolved. Studies of both high dose (100 mg. per day) and low dose (30–50 mg. per day) suggest differences in efficacy between high-dose and low-dose regimens, but these differences are not large (McGlothlin and Anglin 1981b). Dole also believed that addicts had a metabolic deficit that required exogenous opioids in a fashion similar to the need of diabetics for insulin. There is no evidence to substantiate or to reject such a metabolic deficit theory.

The long-range goal of methadone maintenance varies. Some programs are based on a philosophy that affirms indefinite maintenance while other programs aim specifically for short periods of maintenance—that is a few months to two years—and then require an attempt to become drug-free. Currently, no data indicate which of these clinical postures is superior.

S. Sells has divided methadone maintenance programs into those with a high demand for conformity to program guidelines—a patient must have a certain percent of urines free from all nonprescribed drugs and cannot miss treatment days—to programs more lenient about such matters (Sells and Simpson 1976). A typology of programs is difficult to describe because of such policy matters as follows: program demands for behavioral changes; criteria for diagnoses of opioid dependence and admission to treatment; frequency of required urinalyses; administrative and clinical response to frequent illicit drug use as evidenced by positive urines; program policies concerning patient behavior both in and outside of clinics; and pressure to attempt detoxification. Staffing patterns also vary. Some programs are heavily staffed with professionals while others have few professionals and have a high ratio of exaddict counselors. The foregoing list is not exhaustive. Changes in just one of these policies can affect every facet of clinic life and have implications for outcome.

Another dimension on which programs differ is the question of take-home policy. Communities with thousands of patients on methadone maintenance may have a problem with diversion of methadone to illicit use. In places where many addicts are unemployed and in serious socioeconomic need, the street sale of methadone can be appreciable. One of the consequences of diversion is the unsupervised use by persons unaware of the potential of this drug to act synergistically with other intoxicants to produce an overdose. Some communities have therefore created a no-take-home policy. In addition to the diversion problem, there is an occasional death in a child because of failure to safeguard take-home methadone doses from children (Azonow, Paul, and Woolley 1972; Smialek et al. 1977). Childproof caps on take-home bottles partially respond to the problem, but ultimately the addict has responsibility for adequate supervision, as is the case with any other prescribed drug.

Many clinicians feel that no-take-home methadone is a clinically harmful policy in that it causes the many patients who are doing well an unnecessary hardship in getting to programs on a daily basis. Some communities have implemented an experimental policy in which addicts who are doing well are permitted to pick up their methadone at a local pharmacy and only make trips to the clinic on a weekly or monthly basis (Bowden, Maddux, and Esquivel 1976). Programs in some communities and countries permit addicts take-home doses after three to six months of demonstration of favorable progress in treatment. After two or more years of treatment in some countries, some patients are permitted to come to the clinic only once a week and to take home the rest of their daily methadone dose.

One of the complications of methadone maintenance and detoxification therapy is alcohol abuse (Cohen et al. 1982; Kreek

1981). Estimates of the frequency with which this occurs vary widely but there is no question that it is a significant problem. Referral to alcoholism treatment, use of breathalyzer tests, family therapy, and use of disulfiram can be added to the methadone regime. Disulfiram can be used concurrently with methadone with close medical supervision. Alcohol abusers in methadone maintenance tend to abuse other substances more than nonalcohol abusers. Substantial numbers of patients continue to abuse a variety of substances during methadone therapy. This use can be managed by counseling, urine monitoring (Havassy and Hall 1981; Milby et al. 1980), and—if a reasonable period of time elapses without change—by exclusion from the program.

Patients in many methadone maintenance regimens tend to terminate treatment by dropping out. However, they also tend to reenter treatment if readdicted. Sells' group has found that methadone treatment episodes tend to become repeated and that addicts appear to elect methadone maintenance as the number of readmissions grows (Sells 1979; Simpson 1981; Simpson, Joe, and Bracy 1982).

Methadone clinics, like mental health clinics, prison halfway houses, and similar services, are usually not well accepted by surrounding communities. Addiction is a threatening problem and the stereotype of the addict creates public fear. Community relations are, therefore, extremely important in administering a methadone maintenance clinic. The optimal situation is one in which a community or neighborhood has frequent contact with the leadership of a clinic and people from the community have jobs in the clinic. If a community has an economic and social stake in a clinic, community relations are usually smooth. Staff must be trained to discourage the congregation of addicts outside clinics to avoid stimulating community fear and stereotyping. Ideally methadone clinics should be linked with therapeutic communities, halfway houses, and detoxification centers. Multimodality programming increases the ability to serve and is an important public health model for communities with significant opioid related problems (Jaffe 1969). A detailed discussion of staffing and space of a methadone maintenance clinic has been published (Lowinson and Millman 1979).

WITHDRAWAL FROM METHADONE MAINTENANCE

Two different withdrawal regimens are encountered in methadone maintenance clinics. The first is with the successful patient who has a year or two of urine tests negative for all drugs, no alcohol or other drug problem, stable employment, good attendance, and is functioning well within a family. Such a patient will ask about or be asked to consider detoxification. Clinical experience indicates that detoxification is difficult for many addicts. Many lose the gains they have made, but some are able to withdraw successfully and to maintain a drug-free state (Cushman 1981; Senay et al. 1977; Stimmel et al. 1973). Studies on this problem are inadequate in number and in length of the study period. If opioid dependence is a career, then therapeutic intervention must be measured in career terms.

Successful methadone maintenance patients should be advised to attempt detoxification when life stress is as low as possible and they should be advised to expect a regimen taking months or possibly years (Senay 1983). In addition, they should be advised that because of the protracted abstinence syndrome they will need treatment for at least a year or two after reaching zero dose. The clinical principles involved in detoxification from maintenance are identical with the principles described in the following section on use of methadone for withdrawal in addicts dependent on opioids other than methadone. Addicts should be informed that failure to achieve zero dose will not affect their status as patients; the attempt to detoxify carries with it a risk of losing gains such as not using illicit drugs, keeping a job, or maintaining family relationships. These risks should not be compounded by expulsion from the treatment program.

A second category of withdrawal from methadone maintenance is based on administrative criteria. The patient in maintenance may have violated basic program rules. For example, the patient may have been violent or have tried to sell drugs in or near the clinic. One can almost always assume concurrent use of other drugs in these patients. Random urine samples obtained weekly in maintenance clinics usually confirm this use. The withdrawal regimen is usually shortened for these patients in comparison to the regimen employed in the first category of patients discussed earlier. A two- to three- week regimen is humane and usually meets administrative needs.

As in the case of detoxification from street opioids, outcome data observed in follow-up studies on detoxified patients in methadone maintenance are not encouraging (Kleber 1981). In studies of detoxified methadone maintenance patients, Paul Cushman observed a 7.6 percent success rate (Cushman 1981). Success was defined as sustained abstinence from opioids. The methadone maintenance patient with the best chance of achieving and maintaining opioid free status has made good progress in treatment, is employed steadily, has a social life primarily outside the drug world, and has had a long duration of methadone treatment. Those in treatment for three or more years were likely to be abstinent. Those in treatment less than one year are much more likely to resume opioid use. Most clinicians believe, on the basis of the previous studies, as well as clinical experience, that attempts to withdraw successful methadone maintenance patients carry a risk of relapse although some patients are successful. The therapeutic detoxification should be slow. Many patients take over one year or more to detoxify. Alcohol or other drug abuse during this time is a real but not invariable risk (Cushman 1981).

USE OF METHADONE FOR DETOXIFICATION IN OPIOID DEPENDENCE OTHER THAN IN METHADONE MAINTENANCE PATIENTS

Methadone is the opioid of choice for use in detoxification regimens because it is effective orally and because it suppresses the abstinence syndrome for extended periods. The goal of a clinically sound withdrawal regimen is to reduce to a tolerable degree the inevitable opioid withdrawal symptoms. Although some patients can have a symptom-free detoxification, this is unusual. In the last twenty years many workers in the field have moved in the direction of lengthening the time of detoxification treatment. Some of the impetus for the change from older practices stems from everyday clinical experience. Other factors influencing this change have been evidence for a chronic opioid abstinence syndrome (Martin and Jasinski 1969) and clinical research studies stating that slow withdrawal is indicated (Senay et al. 1977).

Research also indicates, as clinicians in diverse cultural settings have observed, that expectation or set is an important factor in producing symptoms during withdrawal. Subjects in one study who were being maintained on daily methadone doses without dose changes and who were blind to their study status, complained of withdrawal symptoms as much as a second blind group of patients who were being withdrawn in small increments.

Clinical experience indicates that it is meaningful to discriminate mild, moderate, and severe degrees of opioid dependence. If dependence is moderate or severe, the clinical course of detoxification requires many months. Symptoms are more severe, and there may not be a successful response to propoxyphene napsylate or other weak opioid agonists or clonidine in the detoxification process. On admission to the withdrawal regimen, the history may help to indicate whether a mild, moderate, or severe degree of dependence is present. Patients who have a pretreatment history of using poor-quality heroin only once or twice a day in the two weeks preceding admission quite frequently have mild degrees of dependence. Addicts who give a history of using potent heroin more than twice a day, on the average, tend to have moderate to severe degrees of opioid dependence (Senay 1983).

When success is defined as the ability to become abstinent and to sustain complete abstinence for any appreciable time, success rates are low (Kleber 1981). Variations in the length of time taken to detoxify patients may cause differences in patient comfort, retention in treatment, and use of illicit opioids. But these differences disappear if one examines status at one year after treatment. Detoxification treatment does not appear to result in permanent changes and is not efficacious for the long term. If one accepts the notion of a career of heroin use defined by repeated recurrence, however, detoxification may be viewed as having a great deal to offer because it reduces illicit drug use, lowers rates of commission of crime, and probably contributes to positive health status for patients if one compares their status with untreated active addicts. Certainly addicts seek detoxification frequently and for some it is the treatment of choice.

A growing body of evidence indicates that the population of heroin addicts applying for treatment can be divided into a least two groups. One group appears not to have any physical dependence on opioids, while the second group distributes itself into subgroups defined by increasingly more severe degrees of dependence. P. Blachly challenged thirty-two applicants for a methadone maintenance program with naloxone and found that 34 percent did not manifest opioid withdrawal symptoms (Blachly et al. 1975). E. Senay and J. Shick found that approximately 25 percent of the sample of 110 applicants to the Illinois Drug Abuse Program showed minimal tolerance to opioids as measured by methadone test dose pupillography (Senay and Shick 1978). R. Wang et al. tested 363 applicants to a methadone maintenance program and found that 59 had minimal response to naloxone challenge (Wang et al. 1974). C. O'Brien et al. found that 15 percent of forty applicants to a methadone maintenance program had no response to naloxone challenge (Raskin 1970).

Such variations in degree of dependence on admission to treatment may explain the disparate experiences with so-called cold turkey detoxifications. If a group of addicts coming for detoxification has a high proportion of minimally dependent patients, cold turkey or nonopioid-assisted detoxification regimens (such as acupuncture, propoxyphene napsylate, clonidine, haloperidol, or other tranquilizers) may appear to be efficacious. However, if the proportion of patients with severe degrees of dependence is high, then cold turkey or nonopioid-assisted detoxification regimens result in needless suffering. It is a common clinical experience that painful withdrawal experiences do not deter addicts from readdiction. Methadone detoxification is the agent of choice if moderate or severe degrees of dependence are present.

Degree of dependence in a given individual may be assessed by observing the effects of administering a known dose of methadone. Naloxone testing or observation of spontaneous withdrawal symptoms in a hospital are other methods. Then one can build a withdrawal regimen on the basis of the clinical observations made. We do not have adequate studies of the role of adjunctive medication in success or failure of methadone-assisted detoxification.

The setting in which detoxification occurs is unquestionably influential in the expression and intensity of opioid withdrawal. Patients in therapeutic communities requiring them to be active and those whose minds are focused on a demanding schedule appear to have much less severe withdrawal symptoms than those withdrawing in a hospital or other less demanding environment. It is important to identify the mental set of patients beginning detoxification. Some deny their perceptions of impending pain and ask to be withdrawn in five days, while others have phobic responses so strong that they cannot think about or discuss the coming experience. Relatively brief clinical management of these mental sets can reduce patients' suffering. It is best for most people to withdraw under blind conditions by setting a date by which zero dose will have been reached and then to reduce doses on a schedule which is not known to the patient. Occasionally, patients want to control their own detoxification. There is no clinical research or experience to suggest that they should not be given permission to do so (Razani et al. 1975).

Clinicians have observed that decrements in methadone doses need to be smaller as the dose approaches zero. Addicts can tolerate reductions of 5 to 10 mg. when their methadone dose is in the 40 to 100 mg. per day range. However, when the 10 to 20 mg. per day dose range is reached, decrements of 5 to 10 mg. are not tolerable. Powerful pressure builds in patients to use illicit opioids. One research group found that decrements of 3 to 10 percent per week are optimal in patient comfort and ability to refrain from using illicit opioids, with 10 percent decrements early in the course of withdrawal and 3 percent decrements per week at the end of the regimen (Senay et al. 1977). The regimen continued over seven months in this research design. Subjects for this study had been stabilized on methadone and were therefore more uniform in their degree of dependence than addicts coming into treatment for the first time. For this reason, extrapolation from this study to ordinary clinical experience may not be valid.

When patients undergoing detoxification report anergia, it signifies that the withdrawal regimen is too fast. If patients experience it, they are impelled to use illicit narcotics. Anergia together with insomnia and bone and muscle aches are the chief symptoms involved in patients' use of illicit opioids during withdrawal. They probably also underlie the use of alcohol and other drugs during the detoxification regimen.

DETOXIFICATION FROM DEPENDENCE ON WEAK OPIOID AGONISTS

If weak opioid agonists, such as codeine or propoxyphene, are associated with dependence, methadone in low doses may be useful in treating the sometimes difficult withdrawal from these drugs (Raskin 1970). Doses used are smaller than those necessary to control withdrawal symptoms from moderate or severe degrees of dependence on strong opioid agonists. The withdrawal regimen is usually shorter in duration.

Clonidine, an alpha adrenergic agonist, will partially relieve opioid abstinence symptoms (Charney et al. 1981). Alpha adrenergic agonist treatment has led to some serious clinical errors. It is generally not understood that patients must cease taking methadone or street narcotics altogether before they start the clonidine regimen. Clonidine and methadone are synergistic for sedative effects so that a combination of slow methadone withdrawal supplemented by concurrently administered clonidine is contraindicated. Clonidine has an abuse potential because of its sedative properties, and street abuse has been reported in the United States.

Some programs attempt to induct addicts into treatment on methadone and then to detoxify them and maintain them on naltrexone (Goldstein 1976). To date compliance with the naltrexone regimen has been a problem (National Research Council on Clinical Evaluation of Narcotic Antagonists 1978). Patients have tended not to take naltrexone over periods of many months or years. Dropout rates in naltrexone treatment have been large and early in the treatment regimen. It is safe in the doses used.

Clinically it is desirable to engage addicts in treatment after they are abstinent because of the protracted abstinence syndrome and because of their need for support and social rehabilitation. Compliance rates are poor because addicts tend to view the achievement of abstinence as the end point of treatment, rather than one step in a continuum of recovery.

METHADONE AND PREGNANCY

The pregnant opioid-dependent patient presents a dilemma because attempts to detoxify her carry substantial risk of death for her fetus (Finnegan 1979a; Finnegan 1979b). Whereas the human adult rarely dies or has convulsions during opioid withdrawal, the human fetus is much more liable to death and to convulsions. Most treatment centers maintain a pregnant opioid-dependent woman through her pregnancy and delivery on methadone doses of less than 25 mg. per day. This regimen reduces the risk of fetal death from withdrawal and also avoids the death of neonates from withdrawal if doses of methadone in excess of 25 mg. per day are used for maintenance through the pregnancy and delivery. When opioid-dependent pregnant women were maintained on 50 to 100 mg. per day of methadone, neonatal mortality increased to an unacceptable level. Loss of neonates is unusual with low-dose maintenance regimens.

With low-dose methadone most neonates experience only mild withdrawal and need no treatment. However, some require treatment with phenobarbital and/or paregoric. Phenobarbital controls hyperactivity and the threat of convulsions, while paregoric controls the gastrointestinal manifestations of the neonatal opioid abstinence syndrome. Other drugs occasionally used are diazepam, chlorpromazine, and methadone.

The human fetus and neonate do not have mature enzyme systems for the biotransformation and excretion of opioids. Consequently, the onset of withdrawal is often delayed in comparison to the adult patient, and the neonatal opioid withdrawal syndrome can last several weeks and be more variable in its presentation. For example, withdrawal may consist solely of hyperactivity or failure to thrive. Common symptoms of opioid withdrawal in neonates are tremor, a high-pitched cry, increased muscle tone, hyperactivity, poor sleep, poor feeding, sweating, mottling, excoriation, and yawning. Less common symptoms include convulsions, fever, vomiting, a markedly hyperactive Moro reflex, and flapping tremor. Gastrointestinal symptoms of watery stools and/or vomiting may predominate. Some clinicians believe that the Sudden Infant Death Syndrome (SIDS) is more frequent in opioid-dependent than in nonopioid-dependent neonates (Pierson, Howard, and Kleber 1972). Close monitoring of dependent neonates is indicated for many weeks, if not months, following birth.

Analgesic needs of the mother can be met with normal doses of usual opioid agonists. As in other medical situations, maintenance methadone does not contribute to analgesic needs. In the event that a pregnant opioid-dependent woman is delivering and has a heroin habit, methadone should be used to control her withdrawal. In this situation, as in other medical conditions, the stress of withdrawal should not be added to the stress of delivery. Usually high stress levels in opioid-dependent women require psychological support, nonjudgmental attitudes, and recognition of their suffering. The mothers' drug dependent treatment needs can be determined once they have healed from any sequelae of giving birth. Withdrawal should not be attempted until their psychologic and biologic status is stable. Although average birth weights of the neonates of methadone maintenance women are greater than those among the offspring of heroin-dependent women, they are still subnormal. If methadone has teratogenic effects or major developmental effects, they are not apparent in the studies carried out to date (Finnegan 1979 a and b).

OPIOID DEPENDENCE AND MEDICAL/SURGICAL ILLNESSES

An opioid-dependent person may sustain injuries requiring hospitalization or may otherwise require medical or surgical treatment. Because opioid withdrawal is stressful under the best of circumstances, it is contraindicated to withdraw a patient when simultaneously undergoing some medical or surgical stress. The principle is not to sum stresses (Senay 1983). Maintenance regimens with methadone are indicated throughout the period of surgical and/or medical treatment. Analgesia can be achieved with normal doses of meperidine, morphine, or other usual opioid analgesics in addition to the methadone required for maintenance purposes. Mary Jane Kreek (1981) points out that analgesia cannot be achieved by simply increasing the dose of methadone used to treat withdrawal probably because methadone has minimal peak effects. Pentazocine or other mixed agonist-antagonists, such as buprenorphine, are contraindicated for analgesia because these antagonists will selectively displace methadone or other opioids, such as heroin, from receptor sites and cause or worsen opioid withdrawal.

In the event that a medical or surgical patient is on methadone maintenance, the dose given in ordinary maintenance should be continued throughout the medical or surgical crisis. When the opioid addict is a so-called street addict, in most cases smooth control can be achieved with 10 to 30 mg. of methadone a day. Methadone is more effective if it is divided into two or three daily doses; but control of withdrawal is adequate with once-a-day administration. If anesthesia is necessary, the fact of concurrent dependence on opioids should be communicated to the anesthesiologist.

Once the medical or surgical crisis has passed, a decision can be made about detoxification. If an addict wants to be detoxified, referral to a drug abuse program is advised. Many patients do not want to be detoxified and want to return to heroin use in their customary surroundings. They should be permitted to do so because it is fruitless to try to detoxify most addicts on a medical or surgical ward. The staff on these wards are not equipped by training or experience to treat addiction. Although an occasional addict may be treated successfully in these surroundings, more often than not management problems occur, such as drug use, intoxication in guests, or stealing. If a patient was on methadone maintenance at admission he or she should be discharged back to the methadone maintenance program without alteration of the dose.

In case of multiple drug dependence—for example, a patient physically dependent on barbiturates, heroin, and alcohol—methadone may be used in combination with one or more central nervous system depressants for safe withdrawal (Senay 1983). If multiple simultaneous dependence occurs concurrent with medical or surgical illness, patients should be stabilized on methadone and a central nervous system depressant such as benzodiazepines and/or barbiturates until the medical or surgical crisis has passed. Withdrawal may then be carried out from the different dependencies either sequentially or concurrently.

PSYCHOLOGICAL ASPECTS OF METHADONE THERAPY

A growing number of studies indicate that opioid-dependent patients have high rates of depressive symptoms when entering methadone maintenance therapy. Methadone does not appear to worsen or to improve these disorders. Patients appear to improve with respect to depression whether they stay in treatment or not (Woody 1977; Woody et al. 1983). Although they improve as a group, rates of depressive symptoms are still elevated in comparison to rates in community samples after months have elapsed since entering treatment.

Recent studies indicate that psychiatric status may be an important factor predicting outcome in opioid-dependent patients. The type of psychopathology, as reflected in Minnesota Multiphasic Personality Inventory profiles, may influence treatment responsiveness (Berzins, Ross, and English 1974). G. Woody emphasized the need for further research investigating psychopathology and psychotherapeutic intervention in addicts (Woody 1983). C. Sheppard et al. found that heroin addicts represented a diverse group in type and degree of psychopathology (Sheppard et al. 1972:). A. McLellan et al. studied both alcoholics and drug addicts in six different treatment programs including a methadone maintenance clinic and found that: "Patients with low psychiatric severity improved in every treatment program. Patients with high psychiatric severity showed virtually no improvement in any treatment. Patients with mid-range psychiatric severity (60 percent of the sample) showed outcome differences from treatment and especially from patient program matches." (McLellan et al. 1982; McLellan et al. 1983).

A number of studies indicate that antidepressants may have a role in methadone maintenance populations. Studies of psychopathology in opioid-dependent persons suggest that depression is frequent in addict populations as is the diagnosis of personality disorders and possibly phobias, but these studies have not been carried out on large samples. Generalizability is, therefore, not established. Addicts in different national settings may differ from each other regarding psychopathology so that cross-cultural studies are needed.

Joe Westermeyer has studied medical and nonmedical treatment methods in the Far East. He has found that Eastern therapies do not differ greatly from Western therapies in effectiveness, although medical therapies including methadone detoxification are becoming more popular (Westermeyer 1979). Again, one must be cautious concerning generalizability.

EVALUATION STUDIES

Critics have rightfully called for studies of methadone under rigorous experimental conditions, with random assignment to no therapy, methadone maintenance, placebo, and/or to a different treatment modality such as a therapeutic community. Attempts to study methadone maintenance under such conditions in Illinois failed because patients would not accept random assignments to therapeutic communities, and insisted on getting methadone maintenance. However R. Newman and W. Whitehill (1979) recruited 100 heroin addicts from Hong Kong for a thirty-two week study. Subjects were hospitalized for two weeks and during this time were stabilized on 60 mg. of methadone a day. Two groups were then formed by random assignment and studied under double-blind conditions. Both groups received the same counseling and the same treatment by an identical staff. One group was withdrawn from methadone at a rate of 1 mg. per day and then was maintained on daily placebo for the remainder of the study; the second group received methadone either in constant dose or was given dose adjustment as would occur in regular practice. Retention in treatment was 76 percent for the methadone group and 10 percent for the placebo group. Use of illicit heroin, as tested for by frequent urine drug analyses utilizing thin layer chromatography, decreased sharply for all subjects who stayed in the study. The rate of conviction for criminal activity was more than twice as great for placebo subjects when compared to methadone subjects.

The findings of the study by Newman and Whitehill reflect those of the Drug Abuse Reporting Project (DARP) and the Treatment Outcome Prospective Study (TOPS), large federally funded evaluations of the national treatment system in the United States (Sells 1979; Craddock 1982). The General Accounting Office of the United States Congress has examined the data contained in the treatment evaluation studies and has recommended to Congress that it direct the National Institute of Drug Abuse to shift more patients into methadone maintenance and therapeutic communities and away from drug-free and detoxification treatment modalities (Report to Congress by the Comptroller General of the United States 1980).

The National Institute on Drug Abuse in the United States has sponsored large nationwide evaluation studies. The largest of these, DARP, has been carried out by Sells and coworkers at Texas Christian University. The data base consists of approximately 44,000 drug abuse treatment clients admitted to treatment between 1969 and 1973 (Sells 1979). Studies on this cohort have now been extended to a six-year period and longer periods of follow-up are projected for the future (Simpson 1981; Simpson, Joe, and Bracy 1982). Stratified random samples taken from the cohort have been studied and given the large size of the cohort, at least a moderate degree of generalizability can be inferred. The DARP findings indicate that over 50 percent of methadone maintenance clients were retained in treatment for one year or more and rates of illicit opioid use and criminality decreased sharply in comparison to pretreatment rates. Employment rates also improved in comparison to pretreatment rates: 39 percent were employed before treatment, and 62 percent of the methadone maintenance clients were employed in the year after leaving treatment (National Institute on Drug Abuse 1981).

A second independent evaluation of a large nationwide cohort was carried out by the National Institute on Drug Abuse which studied 12,000 patients entering treatment from 1979 to 1981. Again, substantial changes were noted in illicit drug use and criminality when pretreatment and posttreatment periods were compared. Employment rates improved a little; because employment was affected negatively by the recession, even modest positive changes are significant. This study added a feature not present in DARP; namely, an evaluation of the psychological status of patients. Depression indicators, found to be high in addicts coming for treatment, improved during treatment in this study. Another finding of both clinical and administrative importance was that clients received many social, vocational, legal, and educational services. In general, clients were quite satisfied with the treatment that they received (Craddock 1982).

Another large evaluation study was carried out on veterans treated for drug abuse in the Veterans Administration Hospital system in the United States. Results of this study essentially mirror the findings of the DARP and TOPS studies: illicit drug use and criminality decreased during treatment and gains were made in social functioning both during and following treatment (McLellan et al. 1982). The findings of these nationwide studies complement those of many city and state reports, including Robert Newman's report in New York City (Newman 1977); Avram Goldstein in Palo Alto (Judson et al. 1980); Senay, et al. (Senay et al. 1973) in Illinois; James Maddux and L. MacDonald in San Antonio (Maddux and McDonald 1973); Burt Associates in New York and Washington, D.C. (Burt Associates, Inc. 1977), and others (Maddux, Williams, and Ziegler 1977; Simpson 1981; Simpson, Joe, and Bracy 1982; National Institute on Drug Abuse 1981; Bewley et al. 1972; Blachly 1970; Bloom and Sudderth 1970; Brown et al. 1973; Cushman 1977; Dupont and Green 1973; Gearing and Schewitzer 1976; Gunne 1983; Kleber 1970; Maslansky 1970; Scott et al. 1973; Shaffet et al. 1980; Tuason and Jones 1974). While not all reports are favorable (Dobbs 1971; Hallgrimsson 1980; Harms 1975; Henderson 1982; Lennard, Epstein, and Rosenthal 1972; McLeod and Priest 1973; Perkins and Bloch 1970), the preponderance of data indicates improved social performance associated with methadone maintenance.

One of the common questions asked, "Is methadone maintenance superior to therapeutic community treatment?" is not answerable because to date it has not been possible to assign addicts randomly to these two methods. R. Bale studied groups of addicts randomly assigned to therapeutic communities or to methadone maintenance and found that compliance with random assignments was poor (Bale et al. 1980).

An important question for the clinician and policymaker is, "How do the two methods complement each other?" The methods may serve two different populations of addicts. An addict with active ties to a relatively healthy family and who possesses a good job may not be an appropriate candidate for a therapeutic community, because engagement with a therapeutic community could mean possible loss of two major assets—job and family. Methadone maintenance or slow detoxification may be a better treatment in such an instance. A heroin addict with no employment, with no family ties, and with social relationships only in the drug culture may be an appropriate candidate for a therapeutic community.

Many methodological problems complicate outcome research. Regression toward the mean, the inevitable dropout problem, and inadequate comparison criteria all need to be considered. James Maddux and Charles Bowden have pointed out that dropouts need to be counted all through the evaluation statistical process so that one is not dealing with "remaining samples." Outcome criteria must be clear and comparison data adequate (Maddux and Bowden 1972). In a study of methadone maintenance patients Maddux and McDonald found that results were still favorable after correcting for these methodologic problems (Maddux and McDonald 1973).

THE UNITED STATES EXPERIENCE

The General Accounting Office (GAO) of the United States Congress reviewed the drug treatment question and methadone treatment in particular. The GAO report cited lack of dissemination of the outcome data as a major problem (Report to the Congress by the Comptroller General of the United States 1980). The data rarely appear in any systematic fashion in articles written in public policy journals or in the media. There are other factors. One is the factionalism in the field of drug abuse treatment. The judgment that providing legal opioids is unethical is still widespread, particularly in the alcoholism treatment community and among therapeutic community workers. Economic factors frequently reinforce the divisions caused by this philosophic split by pitting methadone programs against therapeutic communities in the struggle for survival.

Methadone regulations in the United States have sometimes been too lax and sometimes too strict. Some poorly operated clinics have created justifiable public concern. This has sometimes created a local belief that all methadone programs are ineffective and poorly organized. The disparity between scientific data and public opinion is so wide that some communities in the United States have banned methadone programs (McGlothlin and Anglin 1981a).

In the United States most methadone clinics are located in severely deprived communities. Many people have no experience with the dynamics of disadvantaged communities; therefore, they do not know how easy it is for the best of the efforts to be affected by local needs for autonomy. These needs can create severe tensions between funding agencies and local communities. These tensions can affect maintenance of standards, acceptability of treatment, ability to carry out evaluation studies, and other facets of the operation of a clinic.

Another set of problems stems from an occasional clinic whose operator is so exclusively concerned with profit that the patients and surrounding communities are antagonized. A more serious problem arises from the failure to create adequate standards for training of all personnel involved in treatment of drug abusers. In the United States, the drug abuse field shares this problem with the alcoholism treatment field although the alcoholism field currently is working on the problem more effectively than the drug abuse field.

Another problem with the image of methadone maintenance stems from the nature of the relationship between opioid dependence and criminality (McGlothlin 1979). The high cost of heroin creates the need to steal to support a habit.

The issue of coercion of treatment is as controversial as the use of legal opioids in therapy. The concern usually is that addicts' rights are violated by legal coercion to enter treatment. Coerced patients do as well as voluntary patients.

Still another hurdle for legal opioid substitution is the notion of "cure." It is more accurate to conceive of careers in treatment that reduce crime, improve health, shorten periods of heroin use, reduce time in jail, and lessen contact with the criminal justice system.

To a clinician dealing with recovering patients, community concern over addicts congregating outside a clinic may seem to be overly critical, particularly since the data indicate a sharp drop in criminality during treatment. To the political person attempting to negotiate the demands of legitimate community needs, the concerns over congregation of patients in one area may be of primary importance.

One action which can be taken is to institute training standards for workers in the field. At the present time medical, nursing, social work, psychology, and pharmacy schools do not prepare clinicians adequately to work with substance abusers. Training standards and training substitutions must be created. It is sensible to integrate substance abuse care with standard health care delivery systems, including the existing psychiatric care system.

The medical cost of drug and alcohol abuse, all intoxicants included, is said to approach twenty cents of the health dollar. Integration of substance abuse treatment with standard hospitals and health care seems needed; first, to prevent inappropriate, expensive use of the medical care system; and second, to provide appropriate medical treatment for the many medical conditions that exist in frequent users of alcohol, nicotine, and opioids.

The provision of licensing and accreditation standards for methadone maintenance programs should result in the closer liaison of this form of treatment of opioid dependence with the standard health care systems, including the mental health care system. In the United States there already is some licensing and accreditation, and program regulation has improved to the point where poorly run programs are less frequent.

The technology of legal opioid substitution therapy may improve in the coming decade. We are also gaining a clinical experience with new and adjunctive drugs such as clonidine and newer agonist-antagonists such as buprenorphine. Levo-alpha-acetyl-methadol (LAAM), a long acting congener of methadone, has been extensively used in the United States, although it is not approved for routine use (Jaffe et al. 1972). Compared to methadone under blind conditions, treatment results with LAAM indicate that reduction of drug use and criminality and improvement in social and vocational functioning are identical (Ling and Blaine 1979). From a clinical point of view, LAAM may be effective with a different subset of addicts. Under a LAAM regimen, addicts need only come to the clinic three times a week. They take LAAM on Monday, Wednesday, and Friday with the Friday dose being 10 to 20 percent higher than the Monday/Wednesday dose. Other days of the week can be selected, of course. The provision of long-acting LAAM therapy appears to offer some fiscal and administrative advantages in that staff time can be reduced and more time made free for the provision of direct clinical services with LAAM. Less attention can be focused on drug taking and drug prescribing.

One of the unresolved questions in methadone maintenance programming is the precise role played by the various elements. As the TOPS study demonstrates, programs provide a wide range of services: legal, vocational, and social (Craddock 1982). Patterns of substance abuse are changing in the direction of abuse of multiple substances, in rotating fashion, with new intoxicants added constantly to the mix. Because opioids continue to be abused widely, a role for legal opioid substitution therapy seems assured. Despite its controversial status, legal opioid substitution therapy offers a unique service to some addicts. It will be needed for the foreseeable future in those places where opioid dependence rates are high.

Hopefully, the public and workers in the field will come to appreciate that methadone can be given in subintoxicating doses. Abstinence from other drugs is the goal of a well-run program. Legal methadone is not like "giving bourbon to an alcoholic" because the alcoholic drinks to intoxication. In well-run clinics monitored properly, intoxication-free living with methadone is possible for heretofore untreatable addicts.

THE SWEDISH EXPERIENCE

The first and only state-run program at the University Hospital of Uppsala followed closely the original concept of Dole and Nyswander. J. Erikson and Lars Gunne (1969) first described this program. Erikson (1970) has dealt with the advantages of oral methadone as compared to injectable methadone.

Stability of treatment effect in terms of work rehabilitation over seven years was good: the percentage of rehabilitated patients varied between 59 and 81 percent. To determine the specific effects of methadone maintenance, a randomized comparative study of two groups of patients was carried out. Both groups met the Uppsala criteria for admission to the methadone program. One group was treated with methadone, and the other group was offered drug-free treatment. As compared to the drug-free group, the methadone maintenance group had a lower mortality rate, a higher rate of abstinence from illegal drugs, and better social integration (Gunne and G. Gronbladh 1981).

Another Swedish study compared plasma levels of methadone to therapeutic outcome (Holmstrand, Anggard, and Gunne 1978). During a mean observation period of 33 months, optimal rehabilitation was found in subjects with steady state plasma concentrations above 200 ng/ml. Lower levels of plasma methadone were associated with (1) higher frequency of urines containing illicit drugs, and (2) poorer psychosocial rehabilitation.

M. Scordato (1982) evaluated the Swedish experience with methadone maintenance therapy in 170 heroin addicts treated at Uppsala Psychiatric Clinic This therapy was successful in reducing mortality and permanent disability rates. Addicts in the methadone program were more likely to achieve complete social rehabilitation. Despite much criticism, the pilot study of methadone maintenance was judged to be sufficiently successful to justify its continuation.

THE ENGLISH EXPERIENCE

G. Wiepert et al. (1978) reviewed 575 opiate addicts treated in London clinics between 1968 and 1975. Fifty-two percent were still in opioid maintenance treatment, 28 percent were in the community but not in treatment, 11 percent had died, 6 percent were in custody, and 3 percent had left the country. Some 7 to 8 percent of patients left treatment each year, and the death rate remained at between 2 and 3 percent each year. Heroin maintenance treatment was being gradually replaced by injectable methadone. The percentage of patients with regular jobs improved from 23 percent at entry to 46 percent at follow-up. In 1979 the same authors published data about delinquent behavior in the same group of programs. They found that opioid maintenance treatment had no effect on overall crime rate. Histories of delinquency predicted a poor response to treatment in female, not in male patients.

A. Gordon (1978) reported a four-year follow-up of sixty male patients in a London drug clinic. Forty-three percent had become abstinent, 23 percent remained drug dependent, and 15 percent had died. Ninety-seven percent had previously received a court conviction, and 73 percent had been convicted during the follow-up. Leaving the program within one year of admission was associated with a poor outcome.

A seven-year follow-up of 124 heroin addicts was published by E. Stimson et al. (1978), G. Oppenheimer et al. (1979), and Oppenheimer and Stimson (1982). The results at follow-up were as follows: 43 percent were still attending the clinics, 41 percent had stopped attending the clinics, 12 percent had died, and 5 percent had replaced heroin dependence with other drugs, including alcohol. Only 5 percent were using opiates and not attending a clinic. The results were also presented in the form of life charts. Of total months alive for the entire group, 63 percent of the time was spent in the program on methadone maintenance, 20 percent of the time was spent abstinent, 4 percent in prison, and 3 percent on illegal opiates.

A ten-year follow-up of a representative sample of London heroin addicts was published by R. Wille (1981). After a mean period of fifteen years using heroin, 38 percent were still attending the drug dependence clinics. Almost half of these 38 percent were still being prescribed heroin maintenance; the rest received methadone maintenance. Fifteen percent had died, and 47 percent had stopped attending the clinics. Only one person found to be abstinent during an earlier study had returned to a maintenance program. Those who had stopped taking opioids were more likely than the continuing opioid addicts to have jobs and legitimate sources of income, to be in good health, and to have stable addresses. They were less likely to have problems with the law or contact with addicts. These differences had not been found at the beginning of the treatment in 1969.

R. Hartnoll et al. (1980) published an evaluation of a controlled trial, allocating heroin addicts randomly to injectable heroin maintenance or oral methadone maintenance. The programs were monitored for twelve months. Heroin maintenance was found to be maintaining the status quo, with the majority continuing to inject heroin regularly and to supplement their maintenance heroin prescription with illicit drugs from other sources. Heroin maintenance was associated with a continuing intermediate level of involvement with the drug subculture and criminal activities. Refusal to prescribe heroin maintenance while offering oral methadone produced a confrontational response in patients. This resulted in a higher abstinence rate, but also a greater dependence on illegal sources of drugs for those who continued to inject drugs. Those offered oral methadone tended to polarize between high or low categories of illegal drug use and involvement with the drug subculture, and were more likely to be arrested during the twelve months follow-up. There was no difference between the injectable heroin maintenance groups versus oral methadone maintenance groups in employment, health, or consumption of nonopiate drugs. Refusal to prescribe heroin resulted in a significantly greater dropout of patients from regular treatment.

An attempt to compare twenty-six methadone-maintained patients with sixteen illicit opioid takers was published by R. Paxton et al. (1978). The two groups did not differ in treatment contact, work status, and involvement with other drug takers. There was some evidence that the methadone group was involved in less criminal activity.

Griffith Edwards has written a comprehensive summary of the British experiences (Edwards 1979), providing a balanced view of merits and drawbacks of the British policies and treatment system. The notion that prescribing opiates alone can have preventive effects should be abandoned. The therapeutic effects of the system were considered not to be adequately evaluated. A major shift in maintenance policy is not advocated. More clinical research is needed to provide a basis for future decisions.

THE SWISS EXPERIENCE

A prospective national study on the career of heroin-dependent persons, with follow-up data, has been conducted. These data have permitted a comparison of abstinence-oriented treatment, methadone maintenance, and imprisonment (total cohort n = 248, of whom sixty-three patients were originally in methadone maintenance) (Uchtenhagen and Zimmer-Hofler 1985). Seven years after the first contact, those who were in therapeutic communities or in methadone maintenance relapsed into opioid dependence at a rate of about 30 percent and reached a steady drug-free state in about 40 percent of cases.   The remaining 30 percent are using illegal drugs occasionally, not regularly. Twenty-nine percent of the methadone group were still on methadone after seven years. The rate of cannabis use was lower in the methadone group (30 percent versus 60 percent in the other groups) (Zimmer-Hofler, Uchtenhagen, and Fuchs 1987).   Two-thirds were gainfully employed, and almost two-thirds had steady partners. Delinquency was reduced, but 43 percent had court sentences within the last three years. Among those sent to prison, 36 percent subsequently became readdicted to opioids—slightly more than in the therapeutic community or methadone maintenance.

Three Swiss studies have focused on methadone treatment in private practice. One study was conducted by a private psychiatrist in Geneva, who published an extensive report on his experiences with 243 patients on methadone maintenance (Deglon 1983). One hundred and sixty-two of those had left the program; forty-eight of these were discharged, that is, they did not drop out. These latter with a regular discharge had an abstinence rate of 75 percent with a mean abstinence of 18 months. A study by W. Baur (1983) demonstrated that short-term treatments using methadone almost without exception resulted in long-term methadone maintenance. A third study by R. Weber (1983) evaluated the therapeutic outcome in the same group and documented a considerable stabilization after two years, as assessed by employment, financial situation, stable residence, and absence of delinquent behavior.

Another series of Swiss studies has analyzed various aspects of state-run methadone programs. A study by M. Gmur and T. Hutter (1984) documented a relapse to illicit opioid dependence at a rate of 24 percent. Thirty-eight percent remained on methadone maintenance, and another 38 percent left the program without relapsing to addiction. Many in the entire group were dependent on public welfare, while abandoning their former dependence on illegal sources of income. The process of abandoning illegal drug use during methadone maintenance was analyzed by E. Hermann (1986). Although use of illegal opiates was reduced within the first months, the use of barbiturates soon followed (verified by weekly urinalyses). Those who misused benzodiazepines or cocaine showed practically no decline of this misuse during methadone maintenance. No major increase of alcohol abuse was observed.

Life-style changes occurred within the first two years. Need for social rehabilitation persisted for another one or two years. After this three- to four-year period, a process of stabilization without further progress in social integration and productivity was observed (Zimmer-Hofler, Uchtenhagen and Fuchs 1987). Important factors associated with positive results of treatment were a stable and trusting therapeutic relationship and a well-structured program (including controlled intake of noninjectable methadone, regular urinalyses, and adequate psychosocial care). These findings have been documented by S. Helbling (1986), D. Zimmer-Hofler and A. Tschopp (1986), and A. Erlanger et al. (1987).

Conceptualization and extent of methadone maintenance in Switzerland have been well described (Gmur 1979; Gmur 1981; Gmur and Uchtenhagen 1980). A comprehensive official report on methadone maintenance has been published by the Health Ministry (Uchtenhagen 1984), and a summary of modifications in concept and regulation as a consequence of HIV-epidemiology has been recently published (Uchtenhagen 1988).

THE NETHERLANDS EXPERIENCE

Methadone was first introduced for short-term detoxification purposes. Its effectivity was evaluated, documenting a 25 to 50 percent rate of successful detoxification, although the duration of abstinence was not studied (Kaarsemaker 1982; Van Dalen 1982).

Prescription of methadone by private physicians has led to repeated legal problems and court judgments (Leenen 1984).

Systematic evaluation of methadone maintenance in private practice has not been published.

From 1978 on, methadone maintenance was used as a means to decrease criminal activities rather than to treat addicts. So-called low-threshold methadone maintenance programs were established, putting few demands on participants, with the goal of motivating them into further treatment by bringing them into contact with professionals. This policy has been condemned by M. Kooyman (1984a; 1984b), who has strongly advocated more structured treatment programs. The limited success of methadone maintenance has also been documented in a study by P. Bindels et al. (1982). Based on comparison between U.S. methadone programs and Dutch programs, L. Wever (1985) has strongly advocated official governmental regulation of methadone programs.

THE FEDERAL REPUBLIC OF GERMANY

Publications from the Federal Republic of Germany have been dominated by cautious or negative arguments against the use of methadone. One pilot program established in 1971 and restructured in 1973, was eventually canceled. Eleven participants were accepted into the pilot study, and all were successful according to the original criteria of Dole and Nyswander. Termination of the program forced the detoxification of these eleven subjects. Two years later, only two of the eleven had gained a stable situation (Krach et al. 1978). Recently established pilot projects will be carefully evaluated.

REFERENCES

Azonow R, Paul SD, and Woolley PV. Childhood poisoning: An unfortunate consequence of methadone availability, *J. Amer. Med. Assoc.* 219:321–324, 1972.

Bale RN et al. Therapeutic communities vs. methadone maintenance, *Arch. Gen. Psychiatr.* 37:197, 1980.

Baur W. Empirischer Vergleich von Methadonpatienten mit zeitlich begrentzer und zeitlich unbegrentzer Indikation. Thesis, University of Zurich, 1983.

Berzins JI, Ross WF, and English GE. Subgroups among opiate addicts: A typological investigation, *J. Abnormal Psychology* 83:65–73, 1974.

Bewley TH et al. Maintenance treatment of narcotic addicts (not British nor a system, but working now), *Int. J. Addict.* 7:597–611, 1972.

Bindels P et al. *Effektonderzoek, een onderzoek naar het effekt van het verstrekken van methadon aan heroineverslaafden.* Utrecht: mimeograph report, 1982.

Blachly PH. Progress report on the methadone blockade: Treatment of heroin addicts in Portland. *Northwest Med.* 69:172–176, 1970.

Blachly PH et al. Rapid detoxification from heroin and methadone using naloxone: A model for the study of the opiate abstinence syndrome, in Senay EC (ed.), *Developments in the Field of Drug Abuse.* Cambridge, Mass.: Schenkman, 1975.

Bloom WA Jr and Sudderth EW. Methadone in New Orleans: Patients, problems and police, *Int. J. Addict.* 5:465–487, 1970.

Bowden CL, Maddux JF, and Esquivel M. Methadone dispensing by community pharmacies, *Am. J. Drug Alcohol Abuse* 3:243–254, 1976.

Brown BS et al. Impact of a large-scale narcotics treatment program: A six-month experience, *Int. J. Addict.* 8:49–57, 1973.

Burt Associates, Inc. *Drug Treatment in New York City and Washington, D.C.: Follow-up Studies.* Washington, D.C.: National Institute on Drug Abuse/U.S. Govt. Print. Off., 1977.

Charney DS et al. The clinical use of clonidine in abrupt withdrawal from methadone: Effects on blood pressure and specific signs and symptoms, *Arch. Gen. Psychiat.* 38:1273–1277, 1981.

Christakis G et al. Nutritional status of heroin users enrolled in methadone maintenance, *Natl. Conf. Methadone Treat. Proc.* 1:494–500, 1973.

Cicero TJ et al. Function of the male sex organs in heroin and methadone users, *New England J. Med.* 292:882–887, 1975.

Clinical evaluation of naltrexone treatment of opiate dependent individuals. Report of the National Research Council on Clinical Evaluation of Narcotic Antagonists, *Arch. Gen. Psychiat.* 35:335, 1978.

Cohen M et al. The effect of alcoholism in methadone-maintained persons on productive activity: A randomized control trial, *Alcoholism: Clinical and Experimental Research* 6:358–361, 1982.

Craddock SG. Summary and implications: Client characteristics, behaviors, and treatment outcome: 1980 TOPS admission cohort. Research Triangle Institute Project 23U-1901, 1982.

Cushman P Jr. Ten years of methadone maintenance treatment: Some clinical observations, *Am. J. Drug Alcohol Abuse* 4:543–554, 1977.

Cushman P. Detoxification after methadone maintenance, in Lowinson JH and Ruiz P (eds.), *Substance Abuse: Clinical*

Problems and Perspectives. Baltimore/London: Williams and Wilkins, 1981.

Deglon JJ. Le Traitement a Long Terme des Heroinomanes par la Methadone. Editions Medecine et Hygiene. Geneve, 1982.

Dobbs WH. Methadone treatment of heroin addicts: Early results provide more questions than answers, *J. Amer. Med. Assoc.* 218:1536–1541, 1971.

Dole VP and Nyswander ME. A medical treatment of diacetylmorphine (heroin) addiction, *J. Amer. Med. Assoc.* 193:646–650, 1965.

Dole VP and Nyswander ME. The use of methadone for narcotic blockade, *British J. Addict.* 65:55–57, 1968.

Dupont RL and Green MH. The decline of addiction in the District of Columbia, *Natl. Conf. Methadone Treat. Proc.* 2:1474–1483, 1973.

Edwards G. British policies on opiate addiction: Ten years working of the revised response, and options for the future, *Br. J. Psychiatry* 134:1-13, 1979.

Erikson JH. Methadonbehandling av opiatnarkomaner i Sverige (Methadone treatment of opiate addicts in Sweden). Lakartidningen (Stockholm) 67(8):849-852, 890, 1970.

Erikson JH and Gunne LM. Beroendeframkallande medel (3): morfinism (Dependency causing substances [3]: morphinism). Lakartidningen (Stockholm) 66(48):4992-4996, 1969.

Erlanger A, Haas H, and Baumann H. Therapieerfolg von Methadonpatienten mit unterschiedlicher Indikation, *Drogalkohol* 11:3-15, 1987.

Finnegan LP. *Drug Dependence in Pregnancy: Clinical Management of Mother and Child.* Services Research Monograph Series, DHEW publication number (ADM) 79-678, 1979a.

I nnegan LP. Pathophysiological and behavioural effects of the transplacental transfer of narcotic drugs to the foetuses and neonates of narcotic dependent mothers, *Bulletin on Narcotics* 31 (3&4), 1979b.

C earing FR and Schewitzer MD. An epidemiologic evaluation of long-term methadone maintenance treatment for heroin addiction, *Am. J. of Epidemiology* 100:101-112, 1976.

C nur M. Die Konzeptualisierung der Methadonbehandlung von Heroinabhangigen, *Schweiz Arzte Ztg* 32:1577-1583, 1979.

Gmur M. Die Methadonbehandlung von Heroinfixern: Konzept einer Therapiepolarisierung, *Psychiatr. Prax.* 8:54-59, 1981.

Gmur M and Hutter T. Der 4-Jahresverlauf des Methadonprogrammes in Ambulatorium "Gartenhofstrasse," *Drogalkohol* 3:25-39, 1984.

Gmur M and Uchtenhagen A.   Die Methadonbehandlung von Heroinabhangigen in der Schweiz, *Wschr Prakt. Med.* 30:1228–1235, 1980.

Goldstein A.   Heroin addiction: Sequential treatment employing pharmacological supports, *Arch. Gen. Psychiat.* 33:353, 1976.

Gordon AM.   Drugs and delinquency: A four-year follow-up of drug clinic patients, *Brit. J. Psychiatry* 132:21-26, 1978.

Gritz ER et al.   Physiological and psychological effects of methadone in man, *Arch. Gen. Psychiat.* 32:237-242, 1975.

Gunne LM.   The fate of the Swedish methadone maintenance treatment programme, *Drug and Alcohol Dependence* 1:99-103, 1983.

Gunne LM and Gronbladh L.   The Swedish methadone maintenance program: A controlled study, *Drug Alcohol Depend.* 7:249-256, 1981.

Hallgrimsson O.   Methadone treatment: The Nordic attitude, *J. of Drug Issues, Inc.* 10:463-474, 1980.

Harms E.   Some shortcomings of methadone maintenance, *British J. Addict.* 70:77-81, 1975.

Hartnoll RL et al.   Evaluation of heroin maintenance in controlled trial, *Arch. Gen. Psychiatry* (USA) 37/8:877-884, 1980.

Havassy B and Hall S.   Efficacy of urine monitoring in methadone maintenance, *Am. J. Psychiat.* 138:1497-1500, 1981.

Helbling S.   Therapeutische Aspekte der Methadon-Substitutions behandlung. Thesis, University of Zurich, 1986.

Henderson IWD.   *Chemical Dependence in Canada: A View from the Hill in Problems of Drug Dependence.* Proc. of the 44th Annual Meeting of the Committee on Problems of Drug Dependence, NIDA Research Monograph 43, 1982.

Hermann E.   Der Behandlungsverlauf bei Opiatabhangigen in staatlichen Methadonprogrammen. Thesis, University of Zurich, 1986.

Holmstrand J, Anggard E, and Gunne LM.   Methadone maintenance: plasma levels and therapeutic outcome, *Clin. Pharmacol. Ther.* (USA) 32/2:175-180, 1978.

Jaffe JH.   Experience with the use of methadone in a multimodality program, *Int. J. Addict.* 4:481, 1969.

Jaffe JH and Martin WR.   Narcotic analgesics and antagonists, in Goodman LS and Gilman A (eds.), *The Pharmacologic Basis of Therapeutics.* New York: Macmillan Publishers, 1975.

Jaffe JH et al.   Methadyl acetate vs. methadone: A double-blind study in heroin users, *J. Amer. Med. Assoc.* 222:437-442, 1972.

Judson BA et al.   A follow-up study of heroin addicts five years after first admission to a methadone treatment program, *Drug and Alcohol Dependence* 6:295-313, 1980.

Kaarsemaker F. Evaluatie methadonreductieprogramma CAD Groningen, *Kwartaalberichten F.Z.A.*, Bilthoven, 7:15-19, 1982.

Kelley D, Welch R, and McKnelley W. Methadone maintenance: An assessment of potential fluctuations in behavior between doses, *Int. J. Addict.* 13:1061-1068, 1978.

Kjeldgaard, JM et al. Methadone-induced pulmonary edema, *J. Amer. Med. Assoc.* 218:882-883, 1971.

Kleber HD. The New Haven methadone maintenance program, *Int. J. Addict.* 5:449-463, 1970.

Kleber HD. Detoxification from narcotics, in Lowinson JH and Ruiz P (eds.), *Substance Abuse: Clinical Problems and Perspectives.* Baltimore/London: Williams and Wilkins, 1981.

Kleber HD, Stobetz F, and Mezritz M. *Medical Evaluation of Long-Term Methadone Maintenance Clients.* DHHS publication number (ADM) 81-1029, 1980.

Kooyman M. The drug problem in the Netherlands, *J. Subst. Abuse Treat.* 1(2):125-130, 1984a.

Kooyman M. Naar een consequent heroinebeleid (In favor of a consistent heroin policy), *Tijdschr Alcohol Drugs en Andere Psychotrope Stoffen* 10(4):160-163, 1984b.

Krach C, et al. Ambulantes Therapieprogramm mit methadon, *Niedersachs Arzteblatt* 9:289, 1978.

Kreek MJ. Methadone in treatment: Psychological and pharmacological issues, in Dupont RL, Goldstein A and O'Donnell J (eds.), *Handbook on Drug Abuse.* Washington, D.C.: U.S. Govt. Print. Off., 1979.

Kreek MJ. Medical management of methadone-maintained patients, in Lowinson JH and Ruiz P (eds.), *Substance Abuse: Clinical Problems and Perspectives.* Baltimore/London: Williams and Wilkins, 1981.

Leenen HJ. Het voorschrijven van Opiumwet-middelen door artsen aan verslaafden (Prescription of addictive substances by physicians for addicts), *Tijdschr Alcohol Drugs en Andere Psychotrope Stoffen* 10(4):143-147, 1984.

Lennard HL, Epstein LJ, and Rosenthal MS. The methadone illusion, *Science* 176:881–884, 1972.

Ling W and Blaine SD. The use of LAAM in treatment, in Dupont RL, Goldstein A, O'Donnell J (eds.), *Handbook on Drug Abuse.* Washington, D.C.: U.S. Govt. Print. Off., 1979.

Longwell B et al. Weight gain and edema on methadone maintenance therapy, *Int. J. of Addict.* 14:329-335, 1979.

Lowinson JH and Millman RB. Clinical aspects of methadone maintenance treatment, in Dupont RL, Goldstein A, O'Donnell

J (eds.), *Handbook on Drug Abuse.* Washington, D.C.: U.S. Govt. Print. Off., 1979.

Maddux JF and Bowden CL. Critique of success with methadone maintenance, *Am. J. Psychiat.* 129:440-446, 1972.

Maddux JF and McDonald LK. Status of 100 San Antonio addicts one year after admission to methadone maintenance, *Drug Forum* 2:239-252, 1973.

Maddux JF, Williams TR, and Ziegler JA. Driving records before and during methadone maintenance, *Am. J. Drug Alcohol Abuse* 4(1):91-100, 1977.

Martin WR and Jasinski DR. Psychological parameters of morphine dependence in man—tolerance, early abstinence, protracted abstinence, *J. of Psychiat. Research* 7:9-17, 1969.

Maslansky R. Methadone maintenance programs in Minneapolis, *Int. J. of Addict.* 5:391-405, 1970.

May E. Narcotics addiction and control in Great Britain, *Dealing with Drug Abuse.* New York: Praeger, 1973.

McGlothlin W. Drugs and crime, in Dupont RL, Goldstein A, O'Donnell J (eds.), *Handbook on Drug Abuse.* Washington, D.C.: U.S. Govt. Print. Off., 1979.

McGlothlin WH and Anglin MD. Shutting off methadone: Costs and benefits, *Arch. Gen. Psychiat.* 38:885-892, 1981a.

McGlothlin WH and Anglin MD. Long-term follow-up of clients of high- and low-dose methadone programs, *Arch. Gen. Psychiat.* 38:1055-1063, 1981b.

McLellan AT et al. Is treatment for substance abuse effective? *J. Amer. Med. Assoc.* 247:1423-1428, 1982.

McLellan AT et al. Predicting response to alcohol and drug abuse treatments, *Arch. Gen. Psychiat.* 40(6):620-625, 1983.

McLeod WR and Priest PN. Methadone maintenance in Auckland: The failure of a programme, *Brit. J. Addict.* 68:45-50, 1973.

Milby JB et al. Effectiveness of urine surveillance as an adjunct to outpatient psychotherapy for drug abusers, *Int. J. of Addict.* 15:993-1001, 1980.

Musto DF. *The American Disease.* New Haven: Yale University Press, 1973.

National Institute on Drug Abuse. *Effectiveness of Drug Abuse Treatment Programs,* Treatment Research Report, DHHS publication number (ADM) 81-1143, 1981.

Newman RG. *Methadone Treatment in Narcotic Addiction.* New York: Academic Press, 1977.

Newman RG and Whitehill WB. Double-blind comparison of methadone and placebo maintenance treatments of narcotic addicts in Hong Kong, *Lancet* 11:485-488, 1979.

O'Brien CP et al. Clinical pharmacology of narcotic antagonists,

Annals of the N.Y. Acad. of Science 311:232-240, 1978.

Oppenheimer E and Stimson GV. Seven-year follow-up of heroin addicts: Life histories summarized, *Drug Alcohol Depend.* 9(2):153-159, 1982.

Oppenheimer E, Stimson GV, and Thorley A. Seven-year follow-up of heroin addicts: Abstinence and continued use compared, *Br. Med. J.* 2/6191, 627-630, 1979.

Paxton R, Mullin P, and Beatti J. The effects of methadone maintenance with opioid takers. A review and some findings from one British city, *Br. J. Psychiatry* 132:473-481, 1978.

Perkins ME and Bloch HI. Survey of a methadone maintenance treatment program, *Am. J. Psychiat.* 126:33-40, 1970.

Pierson PS, Howard P, and Kleber HD. Sudden deaths in infants born to methadone-maintained addicts, *J. Amer. Med. Assoc.* 220:1733, 1972.

Raskin NN. Methadone for the pentazocine-dependent patient, *New England J. of Med.* 283:1349, 1970.

Razani J et al. Self-regulated methadone detoxification of heroin addicts, *Arch. Gen. Psychiat.* 32:909-911, 1975.

Report to the Congress by the Comptroller General of the United States, April 14, 1980. Action needed to improve management and effectiveness of drug abuse treatment. U.S. General Accounting Office, HRD-80-32.

Scordato M. 1967-82, unbilancio dell'esperienza Svedese sulla terapia di mantenimento dei morfinodipendenti con il metadone (1967-82, an evaluation of the Swedish experience with maintenance methadone therapy of morphine addicts), *Minerva Med.* 73(47):3353-3358, 1982.

Scott NR et al. Methadone in the Southwest: A three-year follow-up of Chicano heroin addicts, *Am. J. Orthopsychiat.* 43:355-361, 1973.

Sells SB. Treatment effectiveness, in Dupont RL, Goldstein A, O'Donnell J (eds.), *Handbook on Drug Abuse.* Washington, D.C.: U.S. Govt. Print. Off., 1979.

Sells SB and Simpson DD. *The Effectiveness of Drug Abuse Treatment,* Vol. 3. Cambridge, Mass.: Ballinger, 1976.

Senay EC. *Substance Abuse Disorders in Clinical Practice.* Littleton, Mass: John Wright, 1983.

Senay EC et al. Withdrawal from methadone maintenance, *Arch. Gen. Psychiat.* 34:361-376, 1977.

Senay EC et al. IDAP-Five year results, *Natl. Conf. Methadone Treat. Proc.* 2:1437-1464, 1973.

Senay EC and Shick JFE. Pupillography responses to methadone challenge: Aid to diagnosis of opioid dependence, *Drug and Alcohol Dependence* 3:133-138, 1978.

Shaffet A et al. Assessment of treatment outcomes in a drug abuse rehabilitation network: Newark, New Jersey, *Am. J. Drug Alcohol Abuse* 7:141, 1980.

Sheppard C et al. Indications of psychopathology in male narcotic abusers, their effects, and relation to treatment effectiveness, *J. of Psychology* 81:351-360, 1972.

Simpson DD. Treatment for drug abuse: Follow-up outcomes and length of time spent, *Arch. Gen. Psychiat.* 38:875-880, 1981.

Simpson DD, Joe GW, Bracy SA. Six-year follow-up on opioid addicts after admission to treatment, *Arch. Gen. Psychiatr.* 39:1318-1323, 1982.

Smialek JE et al. Methadone deaths in children: A continuing problem, *J. Amer. Med. Assoc.* 238:2516-2517, 1977.

Stimmel BR et al. The prognosis of patients detoxified from methadone maintenance: A follow-up study, *Natl. Conf. Methadone Treat. Proc.* 1:270-274, 1973.

Stimson GV, Oppenheimer E, and Thorley A. Seven-year follow-up of heroin addicts: Drug use and outcome, *Brit. Med. J.* 1:1190–1192, 1978.

Tuason VB and Jones WL. Methadone maintenance treatment: A report on over three years' experience, *Minn. Med.* 57:899–901, 1974.

Uchtenhagen A. Methadonbericht: Suchtmittelersatz in der Behandlung Heroinabhangiger in der Sweitz. Beilage zum Bulletin des Bundesamtes fur Gesundheitswesen. Bern, 1984.

Uchtenhagen A. Zur Behandlung Drogenabhangiger mit Methadon: Zurcherische Richtlinien und Auswertung der Therapieresultate, *PRAXIS* 77:351–355, 1988.

Uchtenhagen A and Zimmer-Hofler D. Heroinabhangige und ihre "normalen" Altersgenossen. Bern: Haupt, 1985.

Van Dalen PR. Ambulante detoxificatie van heroine-verslaafden, *Tijdschr Alcohol Drugs en Andere Psychotrope Stoffen* 8:216, 1982.

Waldron VD, Klint CR, and Seibel JE. Methadone overdose treated with naloxone infusion, *J. Amer. Med. Assoc.* 225:53, 1973.

Wang RIH et al. Rating the presence and severity of opiate dependence, *Cl. Pharmacology and Therapeutics* 16:653–658, 1974.

Weber R. Empirische Katamnese der Methadonbehandlung Opiatabhangiger bei Hausarzten im Kanton Zurich. Thesis, University of Zurich, 1983.

Westermeyer J. Medical and nonmedical treatment for narcotic addicts: A comparative study from Asia, *J. Nerv. and Ment. Dis.* 167:205–211, 1979.

Wever LJ. Effectten van methadone-onderhoudsprogramma's

(Effects of methadone maintenance programs), *Tijdschr Alcohol Drugs en Andere Psychotrope Stoffen* 11(2):86–91, 1985.

Wieland WF and Chambers CD. Two methods of utilizing methadone in the outpatient treatment of narcotic addicts, *Int. J. Addict.* 5:431–438, 1970.

Wiepert GD, Bewley TH, and D'Orban PT. Outcomes for 575 British opiate addicts entering treatment between 1968 and 1970, *Bull. Narc.* (Geneva) 30(1):21–32, 1978.

Wille R. Ten-year follow-up of a representative sample of London heroin addicts: Clinic attendance, abstinence, and mortality, *Br. J. Addict.* 76/3:259–266, 1981.

Woody G. Psychiatric aspects of opiate dependence: Diagnostic and therapeutic issues, in Blaine J and Julius D (eds.), *Psychodynamics of Drug Dependence*, NIDA Research Monograph 12. Washington, D.C.: U.S. Govt. Print. Off., 1977.

Woody GE et al. Psychotherapy for opiate addicts, *Arch. Gen. Psychiat.* 40:639–645, 1983.

Zimmer-Hofler D and Tschopp A. Institutionen fur Heroinabhangige aus der Sicht der Klienten in Ladewig D. (ed.), *Drogen und Alkohol, der aktuelle Stand in der Behandlung Drogen- und Alkoholabhangiger.* Lausanne: ISPA-Press, 24–57, 1986.

Zimmer-Hofler D, Uchtenhagen A, and Fuchs W. Methadon im Prufstand. Forschungsinformationen Serie A, Nr. 8, Sozialpsychiatrischer Dienst. Zurich, 1987.

4

Policy and Practice of Methadone Maintenance: An Analysis of Worldwide Experience

Ambrose Uchtenhagen

Prior to maintenance programs, methadone was first used for the detoxification of opioid-dependent persons soon after World War II. Methadone maintenance as a treatment modality has been closely linked to the epidemiology of heroin dependence; and its introduction in many countries has been linked to a marked rise in prevalence and incidence of opioid dependence. Experimental projects with methadone maintenance were set up in New York and Canada during the early 1960s. Physicians trained with Vincent Dole and Marie Nyswander in New York subsequently established maintenance programs in Sweden (1966), Holland (1968), and other centers in the United States (since 1963). England began initially with heroin maintenance and then added methadone maintenance in 1968. Australia followed with methadone maintenance in 1970; Hong Kong in 1972; Italy and Switzerland in 1975; and France in 1983.

The initiatives for introducing methadone maintenance programs have generally originated from health professionals or from the criminal justice system. Maintenance programs were primarily set up in areas with large numbers of heroin-dependent persons. Initiatives have been motivated by considerable numbers of

This chapter is largely a synthesis of the written country reports published at the University of Minnesota Department of Psychiatry, along with the literature reviews, presentations at the Minneapolis meetings, the discussion at the two Minneapolis meetings, and a later meeting of Uchtenhagen, Arif, and Westermeyer in Zurich.

untreated "street addicts." Other factors favoring methadone maintenance have been negative evaluations of psychotherapeutic treatment for drug dependence and insufficient professional and economic resources to treat this group. Maintenance programs have initially attracted poorer and less educated heroin-dependent persons, but this socioeconomic bias seems not to have been a persistent or widespread one.

SOCIOCULTURAL FACTORS

The ideal goal of drug dependence treatment has been abstinence from drugs. Offering methadone maintenance to attract or enlist addicts into treatment has been a less attractive goal, even when the intent is initially to stabilize their life-styles by eliminating intoxication, withdrawal, and the need to seek drugs. Acceptance of a less-than-ideal initial goal has caused ambivalence and controversy in practically all affected countries. Some countries have adopted, with or without initial experimentation with maintenance, a totally negative attitude (such as West Germany, Austria, and Norway) or at least a discouraging attitude (such as Ireland, France, and Denmark). Others have been liberal or permissive at the beginning. For example, Italy and Spain, initially permissive, produced stricter regulations after negative experiences. Other countries—such as parts of the United States, Holland, and England—continue to have relatively liberal policies but with special regulations governing methadone prescribing. Still other countries have tried to find a pragmatic compromise, admitting maintenance programs, but with rather more restrictive regulations (such as some U.S. programs, Switzerland, and Sweden).

These differences in attitude are partially based on experience, especially experience with negative consequences of permissive attitudes. However, most negative attitudes are probably based on value orientations and ideologies of leading professionals and/or politicians. Their ideologies correspond widely to interpretations of substance dependence, on the basis of such concepts as biological determinism, learning theory, pharmacological principles, and moralistic positions. According to these ideologies, the addict is seen as a nonresponsible victim, a person basically unchangeable, a person prone to be reeducated, or so forth. It is not clear whether sociocultural beliefs determine the decision to establish methadone maintenance, or whether other factors are present. For example, those countries that have decided to introduce methadone maintenance show important differences among themselves in cultural and demographic characteristics. It would be difficult to identify common sociocultural factors among them. Since widespread heroin addiction seems to be the one factor most strongly correlated with methadone maintenance, perhaps the varying national attitudes toward methadone maintenance are epiphenomenal, even rationalizations to support previously made decisions, rather than causal in the decision-making process.

LEGISLATION

All countries included in this volume have repeatedly revised their narcotic legislation before and after the First Single Convention of 1961. Especially in the late 1960s and early 1970s, legislative measures were taken to control the prescription of opioids—methadone and others—to opiate-dependent persons. These amendments include two common characteristics: (1) a required authorization of those programs or professionals who can prescribe opioids to drug-dependent persons; and (2) a central registration of those who are prescribed opiates, as required in, for example, England, Hong Kong, and New York. Nevertheless, there are many differences in detail, as is seen in the following section on regulations.

Analyzing the sequence of legislative changes in some countries reveals a pendulum swing from repressive measures to medical priorities and back again, from permissive to restrictive views and back again. Restriction results from the unwanted side effects of earlier liberal methadone prescribing policies. Easy access to methadone maintenance is advocated to attract larger proportions of the addicted population into treatment. Changes in legislation reflect not only the undesirable side effects of the previous regulations but also changes in the characteristics of opiate use and the size of the addicted population. Large numbers of dropouts from other treatment programs may return to illicit drug using; this can be an additional motive for implementing methadone maintenance for this target group who have failed in abstinence-oriented treatment.

Political decisions in favor of methadone maintenance can be economically inspired. Although costs of methadone maintenance per day are lower than in most other treatment modalities, and lower even than detention, a methadone maintenance program is not necessarily more cost effective than a residential abstinence program. None of the chapters in this volume provide any definite evidence regarding the long-term economic advantages or disadvantages of methadone maintenance versus other therapeutic modalities.

No legislation has yet been established that requires compulsory admission to maintenance treatment. Methadone maintenance is practiced on a voluntary basis only. However, a majority of narcotic laws or criminal laws in the countries represented in this volume provide an opportunity to suspend a sentence in favor of sending an addict to a treatment program. In case the treatment is not followed or otherwise fails, the sentence is to be enforced. In England, Holland, Switzerland, and Italy methadone maintenance is one of the treatment modalities acceptable as an alternative to imprisonment, but only if the drug-dependent person accepts the treatment alternative. The person is still permitted to choose the prison.

Legislation in all the countries represented here provides no maintenance prescription for substances other than opioids. This is due to the predominantly negative effects of prolonged intake of other substances of abuse, such as sedatives, cocaine, or other stimulants.

POLICIES AND REGULATIONS

In most of the countries where methadone maintenance programs have been established and where evaluation has been conducted, some consensus exists regarding the importance of regulations for methadone maintenance. Very few believe today that merely substituting methadone for heroin is sufficient to change a drug-centered life-style and to avoid the consequences of heroin dependence. However, there are great differences in the admission criteria from one place to another, and less difference regarding treatment criteria.

Assessment Procedures and Criteria for Entry into Treatment

The original Dole-Nyswander program selected only candidates with a history of at least four years' heroin dependence, a minimum age of twenty-one, without alcohol or other drug problems, and repeated failure in other treatment modalities. The treatment began with six weeks of hospitalization. The rapid dissemination of methadone programs brought several modifications in these original criteria. Minimal age was reduced, the required duration of heroin dependence was reduced, even experimenters were accepted, and immediate outpatient treatment was adopted.

In 1974 the Narcotic Addict Treatment Act (NATA) became operative in the United States, specifying the criteria for admission as follows:

- current physical dependence on heroin;
- heroin dependence of at least one year before admission, that is, increased tolerance and/or withdrawal;
- addicts younger than eighteen must evidence two detoxifications or other residential treatments;
- no admittance before age sixteen without special permit.

Most of these standards have been described in 1972 by the Food and Drug Administration (FDA), which also stipulated that nobody may be forced to participate in a maintenance program. In 1980, roughly 30,000 persons were newcomers to methadone maintenance in the United States; 17 percent had no prior treatment whatsoever, 0.4 percent were under age twenty. The NATA regulations are still valid as minimal standards; some state regulations in the United States are more restrictive.

Canada put the Narcotic Control Act into operation in 1961, and revised it in 1971, especially for methadone maintenance. The later, more restrictive regulations described a diagnostic procedure, including a series of daily urine testing before admittance to methadone maintenance, as well as daily consultations during the first phase. The new restrictions, including also more severe regulations for treatment procedures, resulted in a considerable drop in the total number of methadone patients. The reasons for the new restrictions were to prevent methadone diversion to the street, to prevent primary methadone dependence, and to prioritize drug-free treatment goals.

Australia has new regulations since 1971 requiring a minimal age of eighteen (exceptions are feasible). Nevertheless, 25 percent had a history of heroin dependency less than one year, 42 percent had never experienced another treatment modality, and 16 percent were minors. This unusual policy of highly liberal methadone maintenance is associated with the relative absence of other treatment approaches, especially abstinence-oriented treatment programs.

The first methadone program in Europe, which was set up in 1966 in Uppsala, Sweden, adopted the original criteria of Dole and Nyswander.

In England, the prescription of opiates including heroin was at the discretion of any physician according to the recommendations of the Rolleston Committee in 1924. In 1965 the Brain Committee restricted the prescription of heroin to specialized clinics but no obligatory criteria were set up for admission.

In Europe, Italy has the lowest age—sixteen years—for methadone maintenance. No prior treatment is required, and in many instances methadone maintenance is the treatment of first choice. Minimal criteria also apply in certain parts of Holland, whereas Denmark reserves methadone maintenance exclusively for the most chronic heroin users. The minimal duration of heroin dependence required for admission is apparently six months (Holland), the maximum three years (Switzerland, where the minimal age is twenty-two, exceptions allowed). These and other national differences can create problems when addicted persons from one country seek methadone treatment in an adjacent country.

In certain programs, court referrals are accepted with informed consent by the patient; in others they are not. The situation is further clouded by conflicting findings regarding the outcome of court referrals.

Dependence on substances other than heroin is grounds for refusing admission to some programs. In other programs, the reduction of polydrug use is one of the first targets in methadone maintenance, rather than a rationale for refusing the patient.

In a number of programs, the presence of physical dependence on heroin is tested by administration of naloxone to precipitate withdrawal. Severe response to naloxone challenge indicates a high degree of physical dependence. This clinical test can also be used to determine the approximate dosage for initiating methadone maintenance.

In most countries and programs, those who provide the treatment decide ultimately about admission to treatment, with the exception of special cases (especially very young patients, where a health authority has to be involved, as in the United States). In Switzerland and other countries, the indications are mostly controlled by appointed specialists who even revise the indications for continued treatment periodically, for example, every six months.

Various screening procedures at intake have been developed and described. The standard requirements are a medical and psychiatric examination and a history of substance abuse and previous treatments. Few programs hospitalize the patients initially for screening and for determining the appropriate dosage of methadone (San Antonio, Uppsala). Other programs assess the patient's opioid dependence through a series of urine testing and the naloxone test as does the Addiction Research Foundation in Toronto. On the other hand, large programs such as Beth Israel Medical Center in New York deliberately do not ask for proof of dependence and start treatment on an outpatient basis. Worldwide, initial hospitalization is infrequently required.

Authorization of Agencies and Individuals to Provide Treatment

As an old medical tradition, in most countries physicians were entitled to prescribe opioids for the treatment of opioid-dependent persons. This tradition previously worked out well with patients dependent on pharmaceutical morphine. Things changed with growing numbers of illicit heroin users. In some countries, such as Ireland, Denmark, England, and Canada, physicians are still entitled to prescribe opiates at their discretion. In Switzerland and other countries, physicians need special authorization to prescribe opioids to opioid-dependent persons. In yet other countries, such as Italy, Hong Kong, Thailand, and the United States, specialized clinics or agencies are exclusively authorized to run maintenance programs. In still other countries, such as Australia, there are specially authorized physicians.

The Federal Republic of Germany had originally authorized a few pilot maintenance projects, and subsequently declared methadone maintenance to be illegal practice. Austria has never had methadone maintenance.

The preference for specialized clinics or agencies has specific reasons. Individual doctors in private practice are more prone to come under pressure from the addict, they cannot offer the whole range of psychosocial services often needed, and they frequently do not have sufficient time to take care of all the psychological and social problems of their methadone patients. Comparative evaluation of agency-run methadone programs and private-practice methadone programs has revealed a better compliance with regulations and better psychosocial care in the agency-run programs of Switzerland. In the light of past experience, methadone maintenance is preferably administered by a multiprofessional team prepared to cover all aspects relevant to stabilization and life-style change.

Staff

Little information is available concerning the staffing of maintenance programs. In most countries and programs, a physician is responsible for prescribing treatment, but formally the physician may only be required for the prescription of the narcotic substance and not for other aspects of treatment planning and implementation.

Certain countries such as Australia have ruled out the administration of methadone by pharmacists to control the daily intake of methadone in the drugstore. In most other countries, administration by pharmacists is a legitimate procedure.

No systematic information is available concerning the staff/patient ratio. In practice, the lowest figures show a proportion of 1:10 (Canada) and 1:13 (Italy), while the highest figures are about 1:50 (certain programs in the United States and Australia). Little is known regarding training and continued education of staff working in methadone maintenance programs. A definite need exists for specialization, training standards, and program accreditation which might be applicable internationally. Recently the Joint Commission for the Accreditation of Hospitals in the United States has developed treatment standards for drug and alcohol treatment, but these apply mostly to medical facilities and are not mandatory. Certification in the substance abuse field (including alcoholism and drug dependence) is now being considered by several professional groups in the United States.

Registration of Patients

To avoid possible enrollment of patients in more than one maintenance program, central registration (municipal, provincial, or national) has been stipulated by law in various countries. England and Hong Kong have national registers, whereas most other countries register their methadone patients on a lower administrative level. Regarding individual patient information, these registers are confidential and give no information concerning individual patients to other agencies, for example, law enforcement agencies.

Dosage and Administration of Methadone

The *initial dose* is calculated to correspond with the antecedent heroin addiction pattern. It is generally 20 to 40 mg., followed by observation. Low doses (20 mg. or less) should be used if there is no definite proof of an existing tolerance for opiates. Subsequent doses over the next four to twenty-four hours depend on the response to the initial dose. If high tolerance is evidenced by naloxone challenge or withdrawal signs, the initial dose may be increased up to 60 mg. daily. Very rarely, a daily dose of 80 to 120 mg. (in several divided doses) may be necessary to abate withdrawal in highly addicted persons.

The *maintenance dosage* varies between 20 and 120 mg. daily. The tendency has been to prescribe maintenance doses of less than 100 mg. in recent years. The original aim of Dole and Nyswander, to block eventual heroin effects by a high maintenance dose of methadone, is no longer pursued in most programs. Italy, France, and Australia limit the maximum maintenance dosage to about 65 mg. daily.

With the exception of England, methadone seems to be exclusively administered by oral intake. Even in England, the initial prescription of injectable methadone has been gradually replaced by oral methadone. Injectable methadone is today used only in Queensland, Australia.

Oral methadone is taken practically everywhere in insoluble form, diluted in syrup or fruit juice, to avoid diversion into illicit intravenous use.

Until stabilization in the patient's psychosocial condition has taken place, methadone is ingested on the premises daily. Take-home methadone doses are admitted in certain programs after a time. For example, U.S. standards permit two days of take-home doses after three months' treatment, three days of take-home doses after two years, and one week of take-home dose after three years, provided there is no evidence for continued illicit drug use, contact with the drug scene, or drug offenses. Similar regulations are in operation in Canada, Australia, and Italy. In Switzerland, take-home doses are avoided by keeping clinics open for long hours.

No common policy exists concerning the active participation of patients in decision making about dosage. Many programs prefer to share information and to have the patient's feedback. Other programs work with blind doses and refuse all discussion or negotiation on dosage.

Concomitant Psychosocial Treatment and Supportive Services

Dole and Nyswander conceived their original maintenance program as a combination of pharmacological treatment and psychosocial treatment. The latter included stabilization of life-style, occupational rehabilitation, and establishment of social contacts outside the drug scene. Nowadays many programs offer supplementary supportive services, such as vocational guidance and training, job placement, sheltered workplace, social support in housing, legal advice, medical and psychiatric care, dental care, leisure activities, and group therapy sessions. The extent and nature of psychosocial treatment and supportive services depend largely on the available resources and the patients' needs. No programs are described in this volume with exclusively pharmacological treatment.

In some programs there is a tendency to provide individual and/or group psychotherapy for all patients. Where patients must accept psychotherapy as a requisite for admittance to the maintenance program, a major selective effect in patient population is expected. Individual psychotherapy is usually provided only for special indications.

Urine Monitoring

Periodic urine monitoring is an essential part of most programs. It aims to detect relapse to opioid use and abuse of other substances. Some programs check urines to discharge polydrug users and relapsed patients from treatment; others perform urine testing to make relapse a central issue for intervention; for example, crisis intervention, teaching the patient about relapse prevention. Detection of polydrug use by analyzing urine samples is also done due to the risk of death from combined methadone maintenance and polydrug abuse.

Various technologies are available for urine testing, such as thin layer chromatography, gas chromatography, mass spectrometry. When evaluating the results of urine analysis, the specificity and accuracy of the technology used has to be taken into consideration. Some methods can give false positive results, especially if other drugs (some licit and some illicit) are in the urine.

In the beginning of treatment, when the risk of relapse to illicit drug use is greater, urine monitoring is more frequent, up to once or twice weekly. With stabilization, the frequency of testing can be reduced gradually to biweekly, monthly, or bimonthly. The range of substances included in the analysis varies as well, for individual patients and from program to program, according to the specific risks of certain patients and to the current drug consumption patterns in the drug area.

Urine testing is prone to unreliability if the source of the specimen cannot be ascertained. Various control methods have been developed. The easiest one is direct observation of the patient during urination. More sophisticated methods include adding easily detectable and harmless substances to the methadone solution, and the temperature of the sample.

No common policy is found with respect to positive findings in urine samples. Whereas some programs exclude patients after a specific number of positive samples, others react with further psychosocial assessment, intensive confrontation, increased frequency of consultations and urine monitoring, or transfer to residential treatment.

The proportion of contaminated urine samples varies with the range of substances being screened in the analysis, with the technology used, and with the characteristics of patients. Only in exceptional cases is there a systematic reporting of positive urine samples. In the countries represented in this volume, the percentage of drug positive urines among methadone maintenance patients ranges from about 5 to 40 percent.

Methadone and Driving

No country nor program reports describe definite rules about permission to drive motor vehicles. Initially methadone maintenance patients are prohibited from driving in some countries because they are under the influence of an addictive substance. In later months or years, arrangements are made to enable patients to drive when they are stabilized medically and socially and when no relapses are detected for a specific period of time, such as six to twelve months.

Methadone Maintenance During Hospitalization and Imprisonment

Patients on methadone maintenance may be hospitalized for various reasons or incarcerated during treatment. Country reports do not state whether maintenance routinely continues under such circumstances. Special arrangements to continue methadone for short-term hospitalization or short-term imprisonment for two or three weeks seem to be common in most places.

The issue merits consideration because hospitalization for somatic or psychiatric illness may be necessary or even urgent in methadone patients. However, the patient who fears the withdrawal syndrome may refuse hospital care. In case of surgical or medical illness necessitating hospitalization, the concomitant stress should not be compounded by additional stress associated with drug withdrawal. It is advisable to continue methadone maintenance during hospitalization, with the exception of hospitalizations due to overdose. In cases of prolonged hospitalization over many weeks or months, a continuation of maintenance may be less useful, or even a disadvantage in some conditions, so that detoxification may be in order.

Methadone maintenance does not create difficulties for surgery and anesthesia. Analgesia in methadone patients may be achieved by adding normal doses of analgesics to the methadone required for maintenance purposes.

When patients have to serve a previous sentence in prison, after being well stabilized in a maintenance program, the continuation of maintenance during imprisonment may be desirable. Detoxification before entering the prison is another solution which may be useful, with resumption of methadone before or soon after discharge from prison. Imprisonment due to delinquent activity while on methadone maintenance creates a different situation. In such instances, programs generally exclude the patient from continuation of methadone maintenance.

Confidentiality

Methadone maintenance goals imply therapist involvement with the social behavior and life-style of the patient. This necessarily involves contacts with relatives, employers, and other key persons, such as probation officers. When the patient is uncomfortable with such contacts, the therapist is in a difficult position. Most country reports do not deal with this issue. Nevertheless, each program has to set up confidentiality policies in accordance with local legal regulations and professional practice. It is advisable to discuss these rules with the patient at the time of admission.

Duration and Termination of Treatment

In most countries where methadone maintenance is an accepted form of treatment for opioid addicts, this treatment is available for an unlimited period of time. We do not know of any country where the duration of methadone maintenance is legally restricted. Some individual programs provide a time-limited change-oriented model rather than an indefinite maintenance model. Such programs attempt to effect a more rapid change than that generally observed in unlimited maintenance programs.

No general rules are evident regarding minimum duration of methadone maintenance. Most programs experience an unrealistic tendency of patients to reduce dosage and to terminate treatment in a couple of months. Those who remain in treatment for more than one year show much better outcomes compared to those who terminate early and drop out of treatment.

The desire to terminate treatment prematurely has various sources. These include patients' (1) unwillingness to accept medication administration under controlled conditions; (2) obligation to report current activities and to provide urine specimens; (3) inability to cope with the challenge of recovery from drug dependence, and (4) unwillingness to give up former contacts and to change daily habits. Rarely do the side effects of methadone lead to premature termination.

Discharge from treatment for cause occurs in all maintenance programs. Reasons for discharge consist of violence on the premises, threat of violence, selling drugs on the premises or in the neighborhood, missing appointments or consultations, being uncooperative with urine testing, excessive or prolonged relapses in opioid use or polydrug use, active involvement in drug peddling, or other continued delinquent activity.

Retention rates in long-term methadone maintenance are mostly over 50 percent for a two- to three-year period. However, dropout rates tend to be greater than rates of regular graduates who are withdrawn from methadone and discharged with staff approval. Rates of expulsion from programs are generally low, under 10 percent.

Most programs have a readmission policy which permits dropouts to reenter the program in case of relapse. In fact, such an experience may become crucial for the intended learning processes in patients who have a tendency to underestimate their risks to readdiction.

Referral of Patients between Programs

A variable proportion of patients are migratory and socially unstable. They move to begin new jobs, to join spouses or new friends, to return home, or to try a new start elsewhere. This may entail a referral to another maintenance program. Problems with this situation are reported from Australia, for example. Problems with referral from one country to another are also reported, from England and the Netherlands, among others.

Special problems exist where maintenance policy and regulations are not unified throughout the country and where major differences exist from program to program or from province to province. The United States and Australia have made efforts toward a national policy. In other countries, voluntary agreements have been initiated on a national level, such as in the Netherlands and in Switzerland. In still other countries, there is a considerable lack of consistency in maintenance policy and regulations. This may be due to a deliberate intention to provide a pluralistic set of maintenance programs for different subpopulations of heroin addicts.

SIDE EFFECTS

Little information is available in the country and program reports concerning the physical and psychological side effects of methadone in the individual patient. Considerable clinical research has been done on this topic. We summarize here the general findings:

Excessive Tolerance. An expressed patient desire for continued increase of dosage is rare. Few patients have had to be excluded from maintenance programs for this reason.

Somatic Complaints. Patients complain of sweating, constipation, impotence, and sleep disturbance. Such symptoms may persist over many months. Rarely do these symptoms lead to a discontinuation of treatment; usually they are overcome by dose reduction. In many cases, however, these so-called side effects are classical opioid effects to which full tolerance has not yet developed during the first six months of methadone maintenance treatment. These effects include the primary opioid effects of euphoria, drowsiness, daytime somnolence, nausea and vomiting, difficulty in urination, edema of the lower extremities, menstrual irregularities, sexual function problems, nighttime insomnia, constipation, and excessive sweating. Inadequate dosage may provoke a daily withdrawal syndrome; this can be overcome by an increased dose of methadone.

There is no evidence that methadone is hepatotoxic or nephrotoxic. Neurological assessments have not revealed any abnormalities which could be attributable to methadone treatment. Adverse medical consequences resulting from methadone maintenance treatment are limited to a few mild drug effects. These effects occur in less than 20 percent of patients, with the exception of increased sweating which occurs in around 50 percent of patients. Serious toxic reactions (such as obstipation requiring medical intervention) are extremely rare.

Numerous studies have demonstrated that the acute administration of short- and long-acting opioids causes various significant biochemical alterations in endocrine and neuroendocrine function. Tolerance develops to most of these neuroendocrine effects during chronic methadone treatment in most patients. However, a few indexes of reproductive endocrinology remain abnormal in some patients during methadone maintenance treatment for longer than one year, such as reduced testosterone plasma levels and reduced sperm counts.

There is a rapid development of tolerance to the analgesic effects of methadone. There is no impairment of pain perception from methadone maintenance.

Psychological Side Effects. Only small amounts of methadone pass the blood-brain barrier. No memory deficits or impaired reaction time due to methadone maintenance have been shown. An analysis of driving records has not indicated an impairment of driving ability. Complaints such as nervousness and lack of concentration are reported. These may be symptoms of incomplete tolerance which abate with time or with moderate dose reduction. Sedation is usually due to inappropriately high dosage, or associated drug abuse.

Pregnancy and Offspring. Methadone crosses the placental barrier and induces opioid dependence in the unborn child. Because this is the same for heroin, the question has been raised as to whether or not such substitution is desirable during pregnancy. There is some evidence for fewer hazards and health risks for mother and child with low dosage methadone maintenance (not exceeding 25 mg. daily) than with street heroin. Detoxification with decreased doses of methadone appears to be less risky than abrupt withdrawal.

During delivery, anesthesia is applicable in normal doses irrespective of methadone maintenance.

Over two-thirds of opioid-exposed infants may undergo a subacute or protracted phase of withdrawal syndrome that could last for months and needs close monitoring. The withdrawal syndrome of the newborn infant is mostly manageable. On the other hand, opioid-exposed infants are frequently lighter in weight and smaller in stature than control children and tend to have sleep disturbances, impulsiveness, hyperactivity, and retardation in walking and speech development. All these effects are reduced with a low dosage methadone regimen during pregnancy.

Genetic Effects. Heroin users exhibit increased levels of chromosome damage which persist for a time after entering methadone maintenance treatment. After one year in methadone treatment, the proportion of cells with chromosome damage declines to control levels. Methadone itself has not produced any detectable increase in chromosome abnormalities.

RISKS

Apart from the somatic and psychological side effects in the individual, methadone maintenance involves a number of risks which concern the larger community and general health policy. These risks can be prevented to a considerable extent by adequate regulations and controls.

First, society must deal with the diversion of legal methadone into the illegal market. This can have consequences such as methadone overdose in the methadone maintenance patient who has been selling doses or else a methadone intoxication or primary dependence from methadone in other individuals who have purchased illicit methadone. This risk is increased wherever take-home policies are not carefully restricted, and where the daily ingestion of methadone on the premises is not sufficiently controlled. Strict ingestion regulations on the premises reduce the risk of methadone diversion.

Another eventual source for a diversion of legal methadone is the patient's simultaneous enrollment in multiple maintenance programs. This is counteracted effectively by central registration of patients. The register method used to identify patients must be sufficiently secure to prevent anyone from attending two or more programs. Central registration, apart from this important practical aim, also provides ongoing information on the number, duration, and location of methadone maintenance patients. This is an important instrument for health authorities to monitor new developments and change. It reduces the risk of methadone maintenance developing into a chaotic and uncontrollable situation. Central registration works only if treatment is contingent on authorization by the central body in which the registration resides. This adds to the bureaucratic complexity and adds to risk of violation of confidentiality. Procedures of the central register have to be organized in a way that ensures accessibility as well as confidentiality, to gain compliance by patients, physicians, and treatment programs.

Several countries have had problems with the compliance of physicians, therapists, and pharmacists. Good intentions alone are not sufficient to reduce the risks inherent in methadone maintenance; rules and regulations must be followed in everyday practice. Such regulations can be practical and still meet the needs of patient confidentiality and early access to treatment. Strategies to ensure efficient and confidential services include adequate training of staff working in maintenance programs, a special liaison service for private physicians and pharmacists participating in methadone maintenance, and individual authorization of every methadone maintenance patient by a consulting specialist. Those professionals unwilling or unable to comply with the regulations must be excluded if education and remedial measures are unsuccessful.

Control of treatment policy, treatment quality, and staff training are less complicated and easier to control where only specialized clinics and agencies are allowed to provide methadone maintenance. Involvement of private doctors and pharmacists adds to the administrative tasks.

Table 1 summarizes the most important problems and risks of methadone maintenance and also the corresponding rules and regulations.

IMPACT ON OTHER TREATMENT MODALITIES

Methadone maintenance programs may have negative effects on abstinence-oriented treatment programs. However, there is little evidence that large numbers of heroin addicts refrain from abstinence treatment when methadone maintenance is available along with adequate regulations for admission and treatment procedures. Extremely liberal methadone prescribing may contribute to addicts' postponing the decision to enter abstinence-oriented treatment, although this has not been demonstrated. On the other hand, heroin addicts may occasionally leave abstinence-oriented programs prematurely because they expect to be admitted to methadone maintenance programs.

Abstinence-oriented programs might feel more entitled to have strict regulations if the patients who drop out from their programs can go into methadone maintenance. However, this effect on residential programs has not been demonstrated. There is no evidence of the impact of maintenance programs on the proportion of imprisoned heroin addicts, although property crime rates often drop for a time after a methadone maintenance program is introduced. Similarly, there is no conclusive study about the impact of the availability of methadone maintenance on the careers of heroin addicts.

COSTS AND FINANCING

The annual costs of a treatment slot in a methadone maintenance program has been calculated in the United States at about U.S.$1,500-2,000 (Illinois), and in Hong Kong at about H.K.$130 or U.S.$30 (in circa 1980 dollar values). These data are useful for

TABLE 1
SIDE EFFECTS/RISKS OF METHADONE MAINTENANCE
AND CORRESPONDING RULES/REGULATIONS

Side Effects	Rules
Excessive tolerance to high opioid dose	Detoxification and restart methadone
Somatic side effects: Autonomous nervous system symptoms, Sleep disturbance	Dose reduction; gradual increase to full dose; time to develop tolerance
Pregnancy	Low dose methadone
Childbirth	Low dose, detoxification
Psychological side effects: Sedation, memory problems, irritability	Dose reduction for high dosage, dose increase if in daily withdrawal

Risks	Regulations and rules
Primary dependence from illicit methadone	Evidence of opioid dependence before starting methadone maintenance
Impeding abstinence-oriented treatment	Require previous abstinence-oriented treatment before methadone maintenance
Concomitant heroin consumption, polydrug use	Periodic urine testing
Diversion of methadone into illegal market, methadone overdose	Controlled intake of non-injectable oral methadone
Enrollment in multiple maintenance programs	Central registration
Unfavorable course of treatment	Concomitant psychosocial treatment and supportive services
Breaking rules and regulations by physician/therapist/pharmacist	Liaison service for private physicians and pharmacists, control of indications for methadone maintenance, exclusion from maintenance practice if noncompliant
Unsatisfactory qualification of maintenance in private practice	Restricting methadone maintenance to specialized clinics and agencies only

cost analysis and comparative cost-benefit analysis only when detailed information is given about what is included in these costs such as consultations, preparation of methadone solution, medical care, psychosocial treatment, psychotherapy, other supportive services, administration, or registration system.

Only limited information is available about financing systems. In many instances, health insurance is available; and in other instances, social security money. Certain programs are free of charge to patients, due to sufficient funding and subsidies.

RESULTS OF TREATMENT

Reports included in this volume give some information on the results of treatment, especially on retention rates, relapse rates, social outcomes and successful detoxification after maintenance. One must consider that these data are hardly comparable, due to a number of differences in sampling, other methodological issues, patient characteristics, and program characteristics. It is evident that methadone maintenance has higher retention rates when compared to abstinence-oriented programs, and it is equally evident that methadone maintenance ordinarily means longer periods in treatment. Ability to work, recovery from drug-related delinquency, and a productive life-style can be achieved during and after methadone maintenance in variable degrees, but in a significant proportion of cases. This evidence is available mainly by comparison of baseline data before initiating treatment and follow-up data during or after termination of treatment. Substantial improvement of health status during methadone maintenance has been demonstrated repeatedly; according to some studies, the mortality figures of methadone patients are considerably lower than those of untreated heroin addicts. Successful detoxification from methadone maintenance occurs in a minority of patients; follow-up studies indicate a maximum of 30 percent successful and lasting detoxification after many years on methadone maintenance.

Limited information is available regarding the specific elements in methadone programs as these are related to outcome, such as dosage (less favorable outcome with insufficient dosage), duration of treatment (maintenance over one year or more is likely to have better results than shorter treatment), and concomitant psychotherapy and supportive services (individualized treatment and support is more effective than standardized treatment for all patients). More information is also needed to determine the role of methadone maintenance in the careers of heroin addicts. It is not known which addicts benefit most from methadone maintenance nor at which stages of their careers they benefit most. It is also doubtful whether the original findings of Dole and Nyswander can be replicated because they attained an improvement rate of about 80 percent—unrealistic for most patients and programs today. There are still claims that a greater proportion of heroin addicts are attracted to methadone maintenance programs as compared to abstinence programs. However, the proportion of treatment slots in various programs, the diverse quality of treatment, and the influence of public opinion, make it difficult to prove or disprove such a statement. In some studies, it is claimed that 5 to 30 percent of known heroin addicts are attracted by maintenance programs. Lack of data regarding the best approach to use with any one patient leads to the conclusion that multimodality programming is the most reasonable approach, that is, methadone maintenance programs with close links to day programs, evening programs, therapeutic communities, abstinence-oriented treatment, and outpatient clinics. Such a multimodality programming can best respond to the changing needs and coping abilities of patients. Any program or treatment system offering methadone maintenance alone should be eschewed.

CONCLUSIONS

The present knowledge regarding methadone maintenance, largely incomplete, cannot be the sole factor in a decision to employ this form of treatment. This decision is and will probably continue to be a political, social, ethical, and legal decision, and not solely a medical or psychiatric one. The extent to which heroin addicts may profit from maintenance programs depends largely on the epidemiological situation, on the availability of other treatment modalities, and on the quality and diversity of the program offering methadone maintenance.

Once the decision is made to introduce methadone maintenance, regulations for admission and treatment procedures should be carefully devised. These regulations, based mostly on clinical experience, must then be closely followed.

5

International Overview and Analysis of Methadone Role

WHO Participants at the Minneapolis Meetings*

Treatment of opioid dependence is usually a prolonged process with repeated efforts to induce changes of life-style rather than a single effort. The common goals of all treatment modalities are to achieve a life-style characterized by productiveness, self-responsibility, adequate social contacts, absence of criminal activities, and absence of drug abuse. As a rule, these common goals are approached by way of a therapeutic contract involving the patient's compliance. A common secondary goal is the reduction of social problems and public expenditures.

METHADONE IN THE TREATMENT CONTEXT

The main difference between maintenance and drug-free treatment modalities concerns the ways and means of achieving these common goals. Drug-free programs ask for immediate abstinence from all intoxicating drugs. Maintenance therapy involves medical administration of the opioid drug while asking the patient to be free from nonmedical substance use.

*Awni Arif (Geneva), James Cooper (Washington), James Maddux (San Antonio), Robert Newman (New York), Jan Ording (Geneva), John Peachey (Toronto), Vichai Poshyachinda (Bangkok), Enrico Tempesta (Rome), A. H. Tuma (Washington), Ambrose Uchtenhagen (Zurich), and Joseph Westermeyer (Minneapolis).

In drug-free programs, abstinence is one of the factors contributing to life-style changes. Similarly, in methadone maintenance programs the supply of methadone is one factor among many aimed at achieving life-style changes.

Patient Populations in Methadone Treatment

It is not always clear if a given opioid-dependent person might be better served by maintenance therapy than by another treatment modality. Candidates for long-term methadone maintenance may be characterized as having a longer career of opioid addiction, having started earlier in life with opioid use, having more previous drug-free treatment experiences without lasting effect, showing more criminal activity, and being older at admission. Drug-free programs are generally recommended for patients at early stages in the opioid-dependent career and for adolescents.

Opioid-dependent persons applying for long-term methadone therapy have to comply with the program's requirements. In some treatment programs there is a specific criterion for previous treatment in drug-free programs before being admitted to long-term methadone therapy.

Special consideration is needed for patients involved in polydrug use. This group creates problems in all treatment modalities, but special problems arise in methadone maintenance due to continued drug abuse. Consequently, some methadone treatment programs exclude polydrug users from admittance.

Methadone maintenance is not an adequate way of inducing changes in life-style as long as intoxicating habits are prolonged by use of various drugs. On the other hand, some opioid-dependent persons can be reached by long-term opioid therapy, whereas they might not be reached in drug-free programs. Some patients in long-term methadone treatment have achieved stabilized lives including employment, material resources, family life, and other adequate social contacts.

Methadone Maintenance and Other Treatment Modalities

Offering methadone maintenance may under certain circumstances distract some patients from other treatment modalities. Patient flow depends on treatment availability, accessibility, and admission criteria. Where failure at previous drug-free treatment is required as a prerequisite for admitting a person to methadone maintenance, this has a significant impact on the treatment system. In settings where methadone maintenance is offered only in larger cities, patients may migrate from other regions to these places. Such migrations have even occurred not only between cities and provinces but also between countries and occasionally between continents.

The presence of long-term methadone treatment may induce changes in the admission criteria and programming of drug-free treatment modalities. They may become more selective, or less tolerant of patients who are not able or willing to cope with stringent requirements. In this sense, long-term methadone therapy may contribute to a more diversified overall treatment system with a wide range of therapeutic approaches.

Nonavailability of Long-Term Methadone Treatment

Consideration of these consequences is not based on direct evidence, and so must remain speculative. However, long-term methadone therapy may reduce illicit drug demand by bringing more people into therapy. Social consequences are related to the magnitude of the problem and the duration of time that opioid dependence has been a serious problem in a country.

Long-Term Methadone Therapy, General Health, and Social Services

Health and social needs of heroin addicts greatly resemble those of other people suffering from chronic relapsing disorders. Existing health and social services can best respond to these needs. To the extent that such services are prepared and willing to provide adequate services to opioid-dependent persons, there need be no separate services for this population.

Short-Term Methadone Treatment of Heroin Addicts

Brief methadone treatment can be a first step in a therapeutic process leading to the life-style changes and freedom from continued abuse of intoxicating substances. Withdrawal treatment should be available even without subsequent commitment for therapeutic programming. However, detoxification alone is no guarantee of recovery. Temporarily reaching zero dose levels does not predict a drug-free life.

Withdrawal treatment can be accomplished by a variety of methods. Methadone treatment is just one of these modalities. Nonpharmacological factors (such as patient expectation and trust, staff attitude, and patient-staff support) are also major factors in withdrawal management, whether or not an opioid is prescribed for the withdrawal illness.

GOALS AND CONCEPTS OF METHADONE TREATMENT

Goals of Methadone Treatment

The principal goal of opioid dependence treatment is the amelioration of suffering and disability through improvement of health and social functioning. This aim applies to the use of methadone as well as to other treatment modalities. Ideally the broadest possible variety of treatment should be available to serve the needs of opioid-dependent persons. To this end, methadone can be used as a therapeutic tool for the treatment of some drug dependent persons. When used for treatment of opioid dependence, methadone should be combined with other treatment approaches according to the individual's needs.

As with other treatment approaches, the specific goals of methadone treatment are (1) the elimination of illicit drug use; (2) the reduction or elimination of drug associated problems; and (3) improvement in the individual's medical, psychological, and social function. With regard to impaired function, this may consist of return to a previous level of adequate coping, or socialization and training up to a new and higher level of adequate coping in a person whose previous skills did not permit that level of function.

Therapeutic goals may be classified as short term or long term. In the short term, decreasing doses of methadone can be prescribed to achieve an early drug-free state (a process often referred to as detoxification). Alternately, stable and continuous doses of methadone may be administered to achieve short-term stabilization without necessarily withdrawing the drug (a process often referred to as maintenance). Long-term goals consist of either a drug-free state (that is, eventual detoxification from the drug) or indefinite treatment with methadone.

Goals may also be conceived as eventual end points, or as intermediate or process goals. For example, an ultimate goal may be the drug-free state. Immediate and intermediate goals can include

(1) attracting the opioid-dependent patient to treatment and alleviating withdrawal symptoms; and (2) retaining the patient in treatment and facilitating a period of stability.

Broader considerations for methadone treatment may be its impact on public health matters with regard to the prevention and control of opioid abuse within the society. In some societies methadone treatment has the aim of reducing criminality and the economic cost of opioid abuse.

The degree to which these goals can be realized depends on the strategic use of methadone along with other treatment approaches. Methadone treatment should be made available only after careful consideration of (1) the nature and extent of the prevailing opioid problem, and (2) the resources that are accessible or can be mobilized.

Concepts in the Use of Methadone in Treatment

The function of methadone in the treatment of opioid-dependent individuals can be conceptualized as follows: Gradually decreasing doses of methadone can be used to relieve the discomfort of opioid withdrawal (methadone detoxification) and to achieve a pharmacologically and psychologically stable state over shorter or longer periods of time (methadone maintenance). There is currently lack of consensus in precisely defining these concepts in time spans; for example, a period regarded as prolonged by some may be seen as short-term maintenance by others.

Methadone alleviates opioid withdrawal distress and presents the recurrent intoxication withdrawal associated with illicit use of short-acting opioids such as heroin. It can thereby facilitate improvement in behavioral and social functioning of patients. Such treatment may also aid in making them more receptive to additional therapeutic interventions.

The following arbitrary terms and definitions for prescribing methadone are suggested:

- short-term detoxification (STD) = decreasing doses over one month or less;
- long-term detoxification (LTD) = decreasing doses over more than one month;
- short-term maintenance (STM) = stable doses over six months or less;
- long-term maintenance (LTM) = stable doses over more than six months.

The following combinations of treatment strategies may occur:

- short-term detoxification;
- long-term detoxification;
- short-term maintenance, followed by short-term detoxification;
- long-term maintenance, followed by long-term detoxification;
- short-term maintenance, followed by long-term detoxification;
- long-term maintenance, followed by short-term detoxification.

The working group recognizes that these definitions are arbitrary and not widely accepted by national laws, nor necessarily by professional practice. For example, in some countries detoxification must be accomplished within fifteen days whereas it can continue over forty-five days elsewhere.

RISKS AND MERITS OF METHADONE TREATMENT FOR OPIOID MAINTENANCE

Pharmacological Considerations

Duration of Action. Given in a single therapeutic parenteral dose to a person not using opioids, the duration of action for methadone approximates that of morphine—a three- or four-hour half-life. However, when given in higher doses to opioid-dependent patients, or given in repeated doses over a period of days and weeks, the duration of methadone action lengthens greatly (whereas that of morphine does not). Thus, it is possible to give only one dose per twenty-four hours and still have little, if any, observable effect from the drug. In the latter situation, relatively little intoxication or euphoria results from the drug, as well as minimal dysphoria and withdrawal effects.

Due to this prolonged action, methadone lends itself both to gradually decreasing dosages (for detoxification), as well as to prolonged administration in stable doses (for maintenance or stabilization). When the medication is discontinued in a dependent patient, an opioid withdrawal syndrome results.

Methadone is cross-tolerant with other opioid compounds, and therefore can be used as a replacement drug. It is a principle of withdrawal treatment that long-acting compounds within a given drug class produce a withdrawal state which is more readily monitored and more stable as compared to short-acting drugs. Unlike some opioid substances, there are no antagonistic properties of methadone, so that administering it does not precipitate a withdrawal syndrome in a person with opioid dependence.

Pharmaceutical Aspects. Methadone can be given orally or parenterally. This is useful, since it may be medically necessary to inject the drug in certain medical or surgical situations. Oral administration in nonemergent situations has practical advantages.

The drug is synthetic, and does not depend on the growing of poppies for its production. This helps in avoiding the diversion from poppies into illicit channels.

Methadone can be produced in large quantities at low cost. It is too complex for a chemist to produce illicitly with simple equipment and materials—another factor important in keeping it out of illicit channels. Because methadone is a highly potent drug, many therapeutic doses can be stored in a small volume, thereby facilitating security measures. It has a long shelf life.

Clinical Aspects. As with other opioid compounds, methadone has relatively few side effects with regular administration in tolerant individuals. Constipation and perspiration are the most frequently reported complaints, with potency problems being less frequent. There is considerable variability among individual patients with regard to side effects, as well as within the same patient over time. All side effects are dose related and reversible. Extensive studies have shown no indications of permanent, long-lasting damage to body tissues. Changes in the central nervous system, referred to broadly as physical opioid dependence, do occur.

Supplying only one dose per day facilitates control over the administration. Thus, patients may be treated on an outpatient basis, returning daily to a clinic or pharmacy for their medication. Early on in treatment, it may be necessary to administer two doses daily until a stable dose has been established. It is easier to calibrate doses with methadone as compared to shorter-acting opioids because the patient is not alternately intoxicated and then in withdrawal as tends to occur with the shorter-acting compounds.

Opium (whether in pill or tincture form) has many of the same advantages as methadone. Its duration of action is considerably longer than the pure products of opium (such as morphine) and many synthetic opioids (such as meperidine). Taken orally, opium has a relatively long duration of action. Withdrawal states can be more easily managed with opium than with morphine and other shorter-acting compounds. Dosage can be given twice a day. It has few side effects similar to those of methadone, is safe for lengthy administration, and produces relatively little intoxication if taken orally (rather than by smoking). On the negative side, the abstinence condition is more severe than with methadone (although

more modified, more delayed, and longer lasting than with
morphine or heroin). Opium can only be taken by mouth or by
smoking; it cannot be injected. Thus, its utility in emergency
medical conditions is limited.

Advantages and Disadvantages of Methadone Treatment

Medical Aspects. In the patient dependent on opioids,
methadone treatment provides relief of the acute withdrawal
symptoms, as well as the subacute withdrawal syndrome which may
persist for months. Craving for opioid drugs is usually alleviated,
although some patients still seek intoxicating experiences with other
drugs. Stable levels of methadone are reached, without detectable
intoxication or withdrawal in most patients. Constipation and
perspiration are frequent complaints, which sometimes require
symptomatic treatment.

If the patient must consume the methadone in a clinic or
pharmacy, this requires daily trips to the facility. This can have a
positive effect by bringing routine contact with treatment personnel
into the patient's daily activities. Or it can be negative if a stabilized
patient must spend a large amount of time or money in daily travel to
a clinic. If methadone can only be used on an inpatient basis due to
legal constraints, this leads to the additional expense of
hospitalization and close medical supervision when outpatient
management might suffice.

Certain benefits not specific to methadone also can result from
methadone treatment. These include the following: abstinence from
impure street drugs; relief from infection, malnutrition,
immunological and endocrine impairment; relief from the economic
demands of purchasing drugs; alternating intoxication and
withdrawal; and possibly alleviation of illegal status or criminal
activities. These same benefits may be realized by successful
treatment with any other treatment modality, so that the issue
becomes one of treatment effectiveness.

Methadone treatment does not necessarily preclude abuse of
other substances. Some patients seek recurrent intoxication with
other drugs, including alcohol, cocaine, amphetamines, barbiturates,
and other substances (including episodic use of high doses of
opioids). This may even involve intravenous administration. The
frequency of this secondary drug dependence problem varies widely
from place to place, being virtually negligible in some times and
places, while affecting a significant minority of patients elsewhere.

Other forms of social deviance, behavioral disorders, and psychosocial problems may persist despite methadone treatment. Methadone alone cannot be expected to eliminate spouse or child abuse, criminality, social alienation, or unemployment. It cannot reverse limitations within the patient (such as social isolation or psychological problems), nor can methadone necessarily reverse common sequelae of opioid dependence itself (such as chronic medical complications, lifelong criminality, or chronic unemployment).

Methadone alone also cannot overcome limitations in the availability of other treatment modalities. Thus, patients as well as clinicians may make greater use of methadone if other treatment modalities are not available or accessible. This becomes a limitation of the treatment system rather than a limitation of methadone treatment.

Finally, patients are apt to become readdicted following discontinuation of methadone, regardless of whether the latter is prescribed for a shorter or longer period. Methadone treatment does not confer a long-lasting guarantee that the patient will not go back to opioid dependence.

A person who uses opioids occasionally, and not previously dependent on opioids, can be made dependent on methadone. This usually results when clinicians are poorly trained, or patient assessments are inadequate. Careful assessment is needed to avoid this untoward consequence.

Fertility in methadone-maintained women of childbearing age tends to be increased over that of women on illicit opioids. This may be due to better nutrition, less infectious disease, less endocrine abnormality, and a more stable life-style.

Ordinarily it is better to withdraw the pregnant woman from opioids, so that the newborn will not enter the neonatal period in withdrawal. However, the desirability of this approach must be weighed against the likelihood of (1) a fetal withdrawal syndrome, and (2) of the mother resuming illicit opioid usage during the pregnancy. In most clinical studies of this topic, the opioid-dependent mothers who are maintained in methadone treatment have better nutrition, less venereal disease, less infectious disorders, and a lower fetal mortality and morbidity than do mothers taken off methadone. The decision regarding the life and health of both the mother and the fetus must be weighed in deciding whether to continue maintenance treatment throughout the pregnancy. There is some morbidity from methadone withdrawal in the newborn during the neonatal period, but rapid and adequate attention to the newborn limits the severity of the withdrawal syndrome. To reduce morbidity in mother and child, the dose of methadone must be closely monitored during pregnancy.

Social Aspects. Methadone treatment frequently facilitates better social functioning in the opioid-dependent patient. It reduces irritability, and can thereby dampen social alienation, interpersonal discord, and impulsive behavior. This may come about directly as a result of the pharmacologic action of the drug, although the psychosocial benefits of associated treatment probably also play a role. Some critics of methadone therapy have expressed the opinion that these behavioral consequences comprise a type of social control by stupefying the patient. In the patient on a stable methadone dose, however, there is little or no evidence of intoxication or stupefication. Methadone treatment may exert its benefits by eliminating, or at least significantly reducing, the cycle of intoxication and withdrawal.

Methadone can also serve as a means of attracting opioid-dependent persons into treatment, especially those who only want physical relief rather than more thoroughgoing psychosocial changes. This can serve as an entree into treatment so that the person, initially attracted into treatment merely for physical relief, may later be amenable to psychosocial interventions and eventual discharge from treatment.

Administration of methadone can provide a time-out period during which the opioid-dependent person does not have to seek illicit drugs, accumulate large sums of money to purchase them, or engage in a criminal or deviant life-style. Proponents of methadone therapy argue that this enhances social freedom, allowing the opioid-dependent person to make decisions about a future life-style free of withdrawal symptoms or anticipated symptoms.

Entry into methadone treatment typically also provides access to other therapeutic resources. Even the brief daily interaction with treatment personnel, who are more socially conforming and integrated into the society, can itself be beneficial. In this way, methadone is sometimes referred to as merely the entree into a broader treatment program.

Methadone may also serve as a reinforcer in contingency management treatment. Just as illicit heroin can reinforce or reward criminality and social alienation, medically prescribed methadone can reinforce socially appropriate coping behavior.

A major problem associated with any outpatient opioid treatment (including methadone, but also other opiates such as opium or morphine) involves illegal diversion from medical channels into illicit channels. This diversion is enhanced by poor security over the drug, overliberal prescribing by physicians, and consumption of the drug outside of medical facilities. As more illegal methadone (or other opioid from medical sources) flows into the community, there may be reduced demand for illicit drugs. This can reduce the flow of illicit drugs into a community, but may also lead to higher prevalence by making opioids more available. Illicit diversion can reduce the cost of opioid drugs, and this can result in less criminality and financial pressure on individuals and families. At the same time, reduced cost can lead to greater availability and experimentation with the drug.

Methadone treatment (or medical treatment with any opioid drug) can lead to popular or political opposition. In some societies, people are morally opposed to the prescribing of an opioid drug to addicts because free availability of these drugs to all citizens does not exist. Drug-dependent persons consequently have a special legal status different from others. Since opioids are an intoxicant in the naive user, their prescription in a medical setting may seem illogical (even though methadone treatment for opioid dependence need produce little or no intoxication). Use of opioids for detoxification may be acceptable socially, whereas maintenance treatment may be opposed because there are no immediate efforts to achieve a drug-free condition.

Following successful use of methadone treatment, there may be pressures to abandon other, perhaps more expensive treatment approaches which do not involve methadone. These other approaches may be highly beneficial in certain patients, or even in many patients at various points in their drug dependence careers.

Methadone maintenance can result in modification of the philosophical and strategic approaches to treatment. There may be less expectation of the patient to change and to modify a problematic life-style. This may come about as a result of an overly simplistic notion that mere provision of methadone to the opioid-dependent person is necessarily going to alleviate all of the psychological and social problems resident in that patient.

Making methadone maintenance available may result in fewer patients entering other forms of treatment, but this has not been demonstrated to date. It has also been suggested that methadone therapy may lengthen the career of drug-dependent patients, presumably by reducing the severity or frequency of crises which might motivate those patients to reverse counterproductive behaviors. It is entirely possible that methadone treatment may augment other treatment approaches and reduce drug careers.

In lengthy methadone maintenance, it has been argued that a form of social control results as the patient becomes dependent on a social institution for the drug supply. Transfer of psychological dependence from a drug subculture or from drugs themselves onto a therapeutic social institution may provide a means for ending a drug dependence career. To reduce untoward social control aspects, some countries have legislated against involuntary methadone treatment.

Certain forms of secondary rewards—for program personnel as well as for patients—can interfere with methadone maintenance. For example, if patients only gain access to special treatment resources (such as legal services or employment training) through taking methadone, that would unfairly promote opioid dependence. If treatment programs are reimbursed only for putting more patients on methadone, rather than treating opioid and drug dependence in a more generic multimodality fashion, that also influences clinicians to recommend methadone treatment.

Methadone cannot reverse social problems which may favor opioid abuse and dependence. These include unemployment, prejudice, or sociocultural disaffection.

Indication for and against Methadone Treatment

Clinical Indications. It is difficult to describe the boundary between detoxification and maintenance treatment. In some countries, detoxification applies to any form of methadone treatment less than twenty-one days, whereas in other countries it may range up to ninety days or longer. Thus, one can refer to shorter and longer durations of methadone treatment. Earlier in this chapter a schema for defining long-term and short-term detoxification, as well as long-term and short-term maintenance has been suggested.

Certain patient characteristics may favor shorter regimens of methadone treatment lasting days to weeks. These include mild physical dependence, shorter duration of opioid dependence, younger age, little or no previous treatment experience, and little or no drug craving or seeking. A clinician would also not want to use this form of treatment if the patient has severe side effects from methadone, or demonstrated little or no ability to collaborate with associated aspects of a treatment program besides the methadone consumption.

The overall severity of the patient's clinical condition must also be taken into account. There may be elements of lesser and greater severity in any particular patient, so that judgment must be applied taking into consideration the complex clinical factors involved. These elements include the type of opioids, the route of administration, and the degree of impairment.

Such decisions for shorter or longer treatment are made on an individual basis by both the patient and the physician. The patient should be well aware of the advantages and disadvantages, as well as side effects and concomitants of both shorter- and longer-term methadone treatment.

Public Health Aspects. If a country does not currently use methadone for the treatment of opioid-dependent persons, there can be valid reasons for not initiating its use. For example, the use of opium for purposes enumerated previously may be more practical, cost effective, or politically desirable than methadone. Alternatively, a country may decide to use methadone treatment in opioid dependence for the reasons elaborated earlier.

Once a decision has been made to treat opioid dependence with opioid drugs (whether methadone or another drug), difficulties may arise if there are dosage limitations or time limitations imposed by legislative rather than medical constraints. Decisions about dose and duration of treatment should reside within the medical profession.

There are also factors which might inveigh against opioid treatment for opioid-dependent patients. These include a very low prevalence of opioid dependence in the population, the ready availability of alternative treatment modalities, as well as high accessibility of these treatments.

If opioid treatment is to be considered for opioid-dependent patients, methadone should be considered as a valuable pharmaceutical agent for the foregoing reasons. It is clearly superior to the shorter-acting opioid drugs, such as morphine. It has certain pharmacologic advantages over opium (whether in tincture or pill form), although there may be socioeconomic considerations which favor the use of the opium over methadone in certain settings.

6

Analysis of Research on Methadone

A. H. Tuma

Researchers of methadone maintenance are aware that scientific investigation of drug abuse and drug dependence, in general, and the study of opioid surrogates for maintenance treatment in particular, may be more difficult to conceive and implement than research in many other areas of health. This is due to the diverse legal, social, moral, and political contexts that may be involved, since they often complicate and confound the investigative process. Despite these difficulties, which tend to inhibit objective and systematic research, an impressive body of data has accumulated over the past two decades on methadone maintenance in the treatment of opioid dependence.

Fortunately, both research data and clinical experience converge satisfactorily in answering a few important questions. First is agreement on the efficacy of methadone maintenance treatment in reducing patients' use of illicit drugs while they stay on methadone and in retaining clients in treatment for longer periods of time than other treatment alternatives. Second, the question of selecting dosage levels has been answered reasonably well for the early stages of treatment. Third, the relative medical safety of methadone maintenance seems to be fairly well established under well-controlled treatment conditions. There are, however, many unanswered and important questions that need to be addressed.

Clearly, a very large number of questions remain open and require further investigation. These include (1) characteristics of individuals most likely to benefit from one or another specific intervention, as well as those not likely to benefit from that or any other interventions; (2) questions of the effectiveness of various drug blood levels in acute and chronic patients; (3) valid criteria for selecting clients for nondrug treatment where abstinence is the designated goal; (4) characteristics of patients who need to be treated with drugs plus counseling and social rehabilitation; (5) duration of methadone maintenance treatment in cases where retention in treatment has been successful and social and occupational adjustments feasible; (6) valid predictors of responsiveness to one or another approaches to treatment; (7) indicators for the use of psychoactive drugs and/or psychotherapeutic strategies in the treatment of psychiatric problems that are concomitant with drug abuse (such as use of behavioral and psychosocial interventions in cases of delinquent and antisocial, violent behavior); (8) the type and magnitude of vocational training that is both feasible and suitable for youth with little or no record of prior educational and occupational effectiveness; (9) the type and magnitude of intervention in the family and social network in which opium users exist and intervention with peer groups in the community.

The universe of the unknowns in the treatment of opiate dependence is very large indeed. Therefore, comprehensive and well-controlled treatment studies are needed to address the range of (1) patient characteristics including history and pattern of drug abuse; (2) treatment variables that target specific aspects of clients' problems; (3) therapist variables; and (4) situational and social context variables. Another issue concerns the generalizability of findings and conclusions based on a study carried out in one socioeconomic and cultural setting to other widely different settings. Most studies in the literature are conceptualized and implemented in communities of one country or state and our knowledge of the cross-cultural validity of some of the findings is limited.

Because the phenomenon of drug abuse is often associated with emotional, social, family, educational, occupational, or legal problems—at least by the time an addict becomes a client, patient, or prisoner—it behooves the communities that have the interest and practical capacity to investigate these and other questions to do so. Simply to adopt or to import treatment practices and policies developed elsewhere is to take on faith a great deal and to assume generalizability of findings where this may not be justifiable. Some of the findings and technologies may well have universal applicability. Other findings may require carefully designed replications to ensure cross-cultural validity.

For example, one of the important issues that must be settled prior to choosing one or another approach to treatment is the specification of the major goals of any treatment program. The goal may be very modest or limited to reducing or stopping the use of illegal drugs. As the goals become more comprehensive and more complex by including either clinical criteria relevant to the mental health of the clients, or social, occupational, and economic criteria relevant to the client's adjustment in society, the nature and scope of the treatment strategies also becomes more complex. At the very least, feasibility studies and cross-validation studies seem indicated especially where the patterns of drug abuse, characteristics of clients, and sociodemographic characteristics of client's family and community are clearly different from those characteristics of the original study sample.

Although considerable progress has been made toward a better understanding of the pathophysiology, pharmacology, and psychopathology of opioid dependence, little is yet known about the etiology of this problem or the biological, psychological, or social markers of vulnerability to it. Fortunately, theoretical and technological advances in the diagnosis of opioid dependence have facilitated large-scale treatment programs and many treatment evaluation studies. The goals of therapeutic interventions and their criteria of success have, however, varied over the past several decades and remain widely different even today from one case to another, one clinic to another, and one community or country to another. We believe that this variation in goals is at least in part due to the fact that so far no specific method or combination of methods have been found to be consistently successful in leading to independence from exogenous opiates—a long-term drug-free state. Perhaps this latter goal is not a realistic or obtainable one in view of the fact that opioid dependence, like many other clinical disorders, is not etiologically homogeneous, that is, not a unitary problem or disorder. Rather, it seems to be a psychophysiological and behavioral end state with multiple and probably interacting determinants. Perhaps with more information about the psychobiological markers of vulnerability and identification of valid risk factors for opioid dependence, including a better understanding of specific roles of genetic and familial factors, more effective and feasible methods of treatment and prevention could be devised. For the present, the goals of our treatment strategies must remain limited and congruent with the state of our knowledge of this condition.

Prevention efforts focusing on the reduction of supplies of opioids, though necessary, have not been visibly successful nor, for that matter, have the educational efforts aimed at inculcating in the young certain attitudes and values with a regard to drug abuse. Whatever the forces that feed, maintain, stimulate, or increase drug dependence in today's society, we have no evidence that efforts at reducing opioid dependence in many parts of the world have been successful. Our hope is that better understanding of etiological and mediating mechanisms of this phenomenon will allow more effective prevention and treatment strategies.

Readers should not expect to find the final word on methadone treatment here. As in all scientific communications, the present reports should be viewed as provisional progress reports that can be useful in the discussion of either proposed treatment programs or future clinical research. The widespread and unquestioned adoption of the research strategies used in these studies for direct application to clinical programs would be premature.

Bibliography

Arnold T and Frietsch R. Zur AIDS-Problematick in der Drogenarbeit: Ergebnisse einer Klientenbefragung, *Suchtgefahren* 233:237–248, 1987.

Azonow R, Paul SD, and Woolley PV. Childhood poisoning: An unfortunate consequence of methadone availability, *J. Amer. Med. Assoc.* 219:321–324, 1972.

Bale RN et al. Therapeutic communities vs. methadone maintenance, *Arch. Gen. Psychiatr.* 37:197, 1980.

Ball JC et al. Reducing the risk of AIDS through methadone maintenance treatment, *J. Health Soc. Behav.* 29:214–226, 1988.

Battjes RJ and Pickens WR (eds.). *Needle Sharing among Intravenous Drug Abusers: National and International Perspectives*, NIDA Research Monograph 80, DHHS publication number (ADM) 88–1567, 1988.

Baur W. Empirischer Vergleich von Methadonpatienten mit zeitlich begrentzer und zeitlich unbegrentzer Indikation. Thesis, University of Zurich, 1983.

Berzins JI, Ross WF, and English GE. Subgroups among opiate addicts: A typological investigation, *J. Abnormal Psychology* 83:65–73, 1974.

Bewley TH et al. Maintenance treatment of narcotic addicts (not British nor a system, but working now), *Int. J. Addict.* 7:597–611, 1972.

Bindels P et al. *Effektonderzoek, een onderzoek naar het effekt van het verstrekken van methadon aan heroineverslaafden.* Utrecht: mimeograph report, 1982.

Blachly PH. Progress report on the methadone blockade: Treatment of heroin addicts in Portland, *Northwest Med* 69:172–176, 1970.

Blachly PH et al. Rapid detoxification from heroin and methadone using naloxone: A model for the study of the opiate abstinence syndrome, in Senay EC (ed.), *Developments in the Field of Drug Abuse.* Cambridge, Mass.: Schenkman, 1975.

Bloom WA Jr and Sudderth EW. Methadone in New Orleans: Patients, problems, and police, *Int. J. Addict.* 5:465–487, 1970.

Bowden CL, Maddux JF, and Esquivel M. Methadone dispensing by community pharmacies, *Am. J. Drug Alcohol Abuse* 3:243–254, 1976.

Brill L. International maintenance programs, in Chambers CD and Brill L (eds.), *Methadone: Experiences and Issues.* New York: Behavioral Publications, 1973, 325–346.

Brown BS et al. Impact of a large-scale narcotics treatment program: A six-month experience, *Int. J. Addict.* 8:49–57, 1973.

Buning ED, van Brussel GHA, and van Senten G. Amsterdam's drug policy and its implications for controlling needle sharing, in Battjes RJ and Pickens RW (eds.), *Needle Sharing among Intravenous Drug Abusers: National and International Perspectives*, NIDA Research Monograph 80, DHHS publication number (ADM) 88–1567, 59–74, 1988.

Burt Associates, Inc. *Drug Treatment in New York City and Washington, D.C.:* Follow-Up Studies. Washington, D.C.: National Institute on Drug Abuse/U.S. Govt. Print. Off., 1977.

Charney DS et al. The clinical use of clonidine in abrupt withdrawal from methadone: Effects on blood pressure and specific signs and symptoms, *Arch. Gen. Psychiat.* 38:1273–1277, 1981.

Christakis G et al. Nutritional status of heroin users enrolled in methadone maintenance, *Natl. Conf. Methadone Treat. Proc.* 1:494–500, 1973.

Cicero TJ et al. Function of the male sex organs in heroin and methadone users, *New England J. Med.* 292:882–887, 1975.

Clinical evaluation of naltrexone treatment of opiate dependent individuals. Report of the National Research Council on Clinical Evaluation of Narcotic Antagonists, *Arch. Gen. Psychiat.* 35:335, 1978.

Cohen M et al. The effect of alcoholism in methadone-maintained persons on productive activity: A randomized control trial, *Alcoholism: Clinical and Experimental Research* 6:358–361, 1982.

Cooper JR, Altman F, and Brown BR (eds.). *Research on the Treatment of Narcotic Addiction: State of the Art.* NIDA

Treatment Research Monograph Series, DHHS publication number (ADM) 83-1281, 1983.

Craddock SG. *Summary and implications: Client characteristics, behaviors, and treatment outcome: 1980 TOPS admission cohort.* North Carolina: Research Triangle Institute Project 23U-1901, 1982.

Cushman P. Ten years of methadone maintenance treatment: Some clinical observations, *Am. J. Drug Alcohol Abuse* 4:543-554, 1977.

Cushman P. Detoxification after methadone maintenance, in Lowinson JH, Ruiz P (eds.), *Substance Abuse: Clinical Problems and Perspectives.* Baltimore/London: Williams and Wilkins, 1981.

Deglon JJ. Le Traitement a Long Terme des Heroinomanes par la Methadone. Editions Medecine et Hygiene. Geneve, 1982.

Des Jarlais DC, Friedman SR, and Hopkins W. Risk reduction for the Acquired Immunodeficiency Syndrome among intravenous drug users, *Annals of Internal Medicine* 103: 755-759, 1985.

Des Jarlais DC et al. The sharing of drug injection equipment and the AIDS epidemic in New York City: The first decade, in Battjes RJ and Pickens RW (eds.), *Needle sharing among Intravenous Drug Abusers: National and International Perspectives,* NIDA Research Monograph 80, DHHS publication number (ADM) 88-1567, 160-175, 1988.

Dobbs WH. Methadone treatment of heroin addicts: Early results provide more questions than answers, *J. Amer. Med. Assoc.* 218:1536-1541, 1971.

Dole VP and Nyswander ME. A medical treatment of diacetylmorphine (heroin) addiction, *J. Amer. Med. Assoc.* 193:646-650, 1965.

Dole VP and Nyswander ME. The use of methadone for narcotic blockade, *British J. Addict.* 65:55-57, 1968.

Drucker E. AIDS and addiction in New York City, *Amer. J. Drug Alcohol Abuse* 12:165-181, 1986.

Dupont RL and Green MH. The decline of addiction in the District of Columbia, *Natl. Conf. Methadone Treat. Proc* 2:1474-1483, 1973.

Edwards G. The British approach to the treatment of heroin addicts, *Yale Law Review* 78:1175, 1966.

Edwards G. British policies on opiate addiction: Ten years working of the revised response, and options for the future, *Br. J. Psychiatry* 134:1-13, 1979.

Erikson JH. Methadonbehandling av opiatnarkomaner i Sverige (Methadone treatment of opiate addicts in Sweden).

Lakartidningen (Stockholm) 67(8):849–852, 890, 1970.

Erikson JH and Gunne LM. Beroendeframkallande medel (3): morfinism (Dependency causing substances [3]: morphinism). Lakartidningen (Stockholm) 66(48):4992–4996, 1969.

Erlanger A, Haas H, and Baumann H. Therapieerfolg von Methadonpatienten mit unterschiedlicher Indikation, *Drogalkohol* 11:3–15, 1987.

Finnegan LP. *Drug Dependence in Pregnancy: Clinical Management of Mother and Child.* Services Research Monograph Series, DHEW publication number (ADM) 79–678, 1979a.

Finnegan LP. Pathophysiological and behavioural effects of the transplacental transfer of narcotic drugs to the foetuses and neonates of narcotic dependent mothers, *Bulletin on Narcotics* XXXI (3&4), 1979b.

Francis D and Chin J. The prevention of Acquired Immunodeficiency Syndrome in the United States, *J. Amer. Med. Assoc.* 257:1357–1360, 1987.

Friedman SR et al. AIDS and self-organization among intravenous drug users, *Int. J. Addict.* 22(3):201–219, 1987.

Gearing FR and Schewitzer MD. An epidemiologic evaluation of long-term methadone maintenance treatment for heroin addiction, *Am. J. of Epidemiology* 100:101–112, 1976.

Ghodse AH, Tregenza G, and Li M. Effect of fear of AIDS on sharing of injection equipment among drug abusers, *Brit. Med. J.* 295:698–699, 1987.

Gmur M. Die Konzeptualisierung der Methadonbehandlung von Heroinabhangigen, *Schweiz Arzte Ztg* 32:1577–1583, 1979.

Gmur M. Die Methadonbehandlung von Heroinfixern: Konzept einer Therapiepolarisierung, *Psychiatr. Prax.* 8:54–59, 1981.

Gmur M and Hutter T. Der 4-Jahresverlauf des Methadonprogrammes in Ambulatorium "Gartenhofstrasse," *Drogalkohol* 3:25–39, 1984.

Gmur M and Uchtenhagen A. Die Methadonbehandlung von Heroinabhangigen in der Schweiz, *Wschr Prakt. Med.* 30:1228–1235, 1980.

Goldstein A. Heroin addiction: Sequential treatment employing pharmacological supports, *Arch. Gen. Psychiat.* 33:353, 1976.

Gordon AM. Drugs and delinquency: A four-year follow-up of drug clinic patients, *Brit. J. Psychiatry* 132:21–26, 1978.

Gritz ER et al. Physiological and psychological effects of methadone in man, *Arch. Gen. Psychiat.* 32:237–242, 1975.

Gunne LM. The fate of the Swedish methadone maintenance treatment programme, *Drug Alcohol Depend.* 1:99–103, 1983.

Gunne LM and Gronbladh L. The Swedish methadone maintenance program: A controlled study, *Drug Alcohol Depend.* 7:249–256, 1981.

Haas H and Kurz T. Psychische auswirkungen des HIV-Tests bei drogenabhangigen, *Schweiz Rundschau Med (PRAXIS)* 77/21:582–586, 1988.

Hallgrimsson O. Methadone treatment: The Nordic attitude, *J. of Drug Issues, Inc.* 10:463–474, 1980.

Harms E. Some shortcomings of methadone maintenance, *British J. Addict*. 70:77–81, 1975.

Harms G et al. Risk factors for HIV infection in German I.V. drug users, *Klin. Wochenschr.* 65:376–379, 1987.

Hartnoll RL et al. Evaluation of heroin maintenance in controlled trial, *Arch. Gen. Psychiatry* (USA) 37/8:877–884, 1980.

Havassy B and Hall S. Efficacy of urine monitoring in methadone maintenance, *Am. J. Psychiat.* 138:1497–1500, 1981.

Helbling S. Therapeutische Aspekte der Methadon-Substitutions behandlung. Thesis, University of Zurich, 1986.

Henderson IWD. *Chemical Dependence in Canada: A View from the Hill in Problems of Drug Dependence.* Proc. of the 44th Annual Meeting of the Committee on Problems of Drug Dependence, NIDA Research Monograph 43, 1982.

Hermann E. Der Behandlungsverlauf bei Opiatabhangigen in staatlichen Methadonprogrammen. Thesis, University of Zurich, 1986.

Holmstrand J, Anggard E, and Gunne LM. Methadone maintenance: plasma levels and therapeutic outcome, *Clin. Pharmacol. Ther.* (USA) 32/2:175–180, 1978.

Hopkins W. Needle sharing and street behavior in response to AIDS in New York City, in Battjes RJ and Pickens RW (eds.), *Needle Sharing among Intravenous Drug Abusers: National and International Perspectives,* NIDA Research Monograph 80, DHHS publication number (ADM) 88-1567, 1988.

Huber-Stemich F and Haas H. Pravention der HIV-infektion im methadonprogramm, *Sozialpsychiatrischer Dienst der Psychiatrischen Universitatsklinik Zurich (zur Publikation vorgesehen,* 1989).

Hummel RF et al. (eds.). *AIDS: Impact on Public Policy.* New York: Plenum Press, 1986.

Jaffe JH. Experience with the use of methadone in a multimodality program, *Int. J. Addict.* 4:481, 1969.

Jaffe JH and Martin WR. Narcotic analgesics and antagonists, in Goodman LS, and Gilman A, (eds.), *The Pharmacologic Basis of Therapeutics.* New York: Macmillan Publishers, 1975.

Jaffe JH et al. Methadyl acetate vs. methadone: A double-blind study in heroin users, *J. Amer. Med. Assoc.* 222:437–442, 1972.

Judson BA et al. A follow-up study of heroin addicts five years after first admission to a methadone treatment program, *Drug Alcohol Depend.* 6:295–313, 1980.

Kaarsemaker F. Evaluatie methadonreductieprogramma CAD Groningen, *Kwartaalberichten F.Z.A.*, Bilthoven, 7:15–19, 1982.

Kelley D, Welch R, and McKnelley W. Methadone maintenance: An assessment of potential fluctuations in behavior between doses, *Int. J. Addict.* 13:1061–1068, 1978.

Kjeldgaard JM et al. Methadone-induced pulmonary edema, *J. Amer. Med. Assoc.* 218:882–883, 1971.

Kleber HD. The New Haven methadone maintenance program, *Int. J. Addict.* 5:449–463, 1970.

Kleber HD. Detoxification from narcotics, in Lowinson JH and Ruiz P (eds.), *Substance Abuse: Clinical Problems and Perspectives.* Baltimore/London: Williams and Wilkins, 1981.

Kleber HD, Stobetz F, and Mezritz M. *Medical Evaluation of Long-Term Methadone Maintenance Clients.* DHHS publication number (ADM) 81–1029, 1980.

Kooyman M. The drug problem in the Netherlands, *J. Subst. Abuse Treat.* 1(2):125–130, 1984a.

Kooyman M. Naar een consequent heroinebeleid (In favor of a consistent heroin policy), *Tijdschr Alcohol Drugs en Andere Psychotrope Stoffen* 10(4):160–163, 1984b.

Krach C et al. Ambulantes Therapieprogramm mit methadon, *Niedersachs Arzteblatt* 9:289, 1978.

Kreek MJ. Methadone in treatment: Psychological and pharmacological issues, in Dupont RL, Goldstein A, and O'Donnell J (eds.), *Handbook on Drug Abuse.* Washington, D.C.: U.S. Govt. Print. Off., 1979.

Kreek MJ. Medical management of methadone-maintained patients, in Lowinson JH and Ruiz P (eds.), *Substance Abuse: Clinical Problems and Perspectives.* Baltimore/London: Williams and Wilkins, 1981.

Leenen HJ. Het voorschrijven van Opiumwet-middelen door artsen aan verslaafden (Prescription of addictive substances by physicians for addicts), *Tijdschr Alcohol Drugs en Andere Psychotrope Stoffen* 10(4):143–147, 1984.

Lennard HL, Epstein LJ, and Rosenthal MS. The methadone illusion, *Science* 176:881–884, 1972.

Ling W and Blaine SD. The use of LAAM in treatment, in Dupont RL, Goldstein A, and O'Donnell J (eds.), *Handbook on Drug*

Abuse. Washington, D.C.: U.S. Govt. Print. Off., 1979.

Longwell B et al. Weight gain and edema on methadone maintenance therapy, *Int. J. of Addict.* 14:329–335, 1979.

Lowinson JH and Millman RB. Clinical aspects of methadone maintenance treatment, in Dupont RL, Goldstein A, and O'Donnell J (eds.), *Handbook on Drug Abuse.* Washington, D.C.: U.S. Govt. Print. Off., 1979.

Maddux JF and Bowden CL. Critique of success with methadone maintenance, *Am. J. Psychiat.* 129:440–446, 1972.

Maddux JF and McDonald LK. Status of 100 San Antonio addicts one year after admission to methadone maintenance, *Drug Forum* 2:239–252, 1973.

Maddux JF, Williams TR, and Ziegler JA. Driving records before and during methadone maintenance, *Am. J. Drug Alcohol Abuse:* 4(1):91–100, 1977.

Mann J. AIDS, *World Health Forum* 8:361–370, 1987.

Martin WR and Jasinski DR. Psychological parameters of morphine dependence in man: Tolerance, early abstinence, protracted abstinence, *J. of Psychiat. Research* 7:9–17, 1969.

Maslansky R. Methadone maintenance programs in Minneapolis, *Int. J. of Addict.* 5:391–405, 1970.

May E. Narcotics addiction and control in Great Britain, *Dealing with Drug Abuse.* New York: Praeger, 1973.

McGlothlin W. Drugs and crime, in Dupont RL, Goldstein A, and O'Donnell J (eds.), *Handbook on Drug Abuse.* Washington, D.C.: U.S. Govt. Print. Off., 1979.

McGlothlin WH and Anglin MD. Shutting off methadone: Costs and benefits, *Arch. Gen. Psychiat.* 38:885–892, 1981a.

McGlothlin WH and Anglin MD. Long-term follow-up of clients of high- and low-dose methadone programs, *Arch. Gen. Psychiat.* 38:1055–1063, 1981b.

McLellan AT et al. Is treatment for substance abuse effective? *J. Amer. Med. Assoc.* 247:1423–1428, 1982.

McLellan AT et al. Predicting response to alcohol and drug abuse treatments, *Arch. Gen. Psychiat.* 40(6):620–625, 1983.

McLeod WR and Priest PN. Methadone maintenance in Auckland: The failure of a programme, *Brit. J. Addict.* 68:45–50, 1973.

Milby JB et al. Effectiveness of urine surveillance as an adjunct to outpatient psychotherapy for drug abusers, *Int. J. of Addict.* 15:993–1001, 1980.

Mondanaro J. Strategies for AIDS-prevention: Motivation health behavior in drug-dependent women, *J. of Psychoactive Drugs* 19(2):143–150, 1987.

Musto DF. *The American Disease.* New Haven: Yale University Press, 1973.

National Institute on Drug Abuse. *Effectiveness of Drug Abuse Treatment Programs,* Treatment Research Report, DHHS publication number (ADM) 81-1143, 1981.

Newman RG. *Methadone Treatment in Narcotic Addiction.* New York: Academic Press, 1977.

Newman RG and Whitehill WB. Double-blind comparison of methadone and placebo maintenance treatments of narcotic addicts in Hong Kong, *Lancet* 11:485-488, 1979.

Newmeyer JA. Why bleach? Development of a strategy to combat HIV contagion among San Francisco intravenous drug users, in Battjes RJ and Pickens RW (eds.), *Needle Sharing among Intravenous Drug Abusers: National and International Perspectives,* NIDA Research Monograph 80, DHHS publication number (ADM) 88-1567, 151-159, 1988.

Novick DM et al. Abstract of clinical research findings: Therapeutic and historical aspects, in Harris LS (ed.), *Problems of Drug Dependence (1985),* NIDA Research Monograph Series 67, 318-320, 1986.

O'Brien CP et al. Clinical pharmacology of narcotic antagonists, *Annals of the N.Y. Acad. of Science* 311:232-240, 1978.

Oppenheimer E and Stimson GV. Seven-year follow-up of heroin addicts: Life histories summarized, *Drug Alcohol Depend.* 9(2):153-159, 1982.

Oppenheimer E, Stimson GV, and Thorley A. Seven-year follow-up of heroin addicts: Abstinence and continued use compared, *Br. Med. J.* 2/6191, 627-630, 1979.

Paxton R, Mullin P, and Beatti J. The effects of methadone maintenance with opioid takers: A review and some findings from one British city, *Br. J. Psychiatry* 132:473-481, 1978.

Perkins ME and Bloch HI. Survey of a methadone maintenance treatment program, *Am. J. Psychiat.* 126:33-40, 1970.

Pierson PS, Howard P, and Kleber HD. Sudden deaths in infants born to methadone-maintained addicts, *J. Amer. Med. Assoc.* 220:1733, 1972.

Power RM. The influence of AIDS upon patterns of intravenous use: Syringe and needle sharing among illicit drug users in Britain, in Battjes RJ and Pickens RW (eds.), *Needle Sharing among Intravenous Drug Abusers: National and International Perspectives,* NIDA Research Monograph 80, DHHS publication number (ADM) 88-1567, 75-88, 1988.

Quinn TC et al. AIDS in Africa: An epidemiologic paradigm, *Science* 234:955-963, 1986.

Raskin NN. Methadone for the pentazocine-dependent patient, *New England J. of Med.* 283:1349, 1970.

Razani J et al. Self-regulated methadone detoxification of heroin addicts, *Arch. Gen. Psychiat.* 32:909–911, 1975.

Report to the Congress by the Comptroller General of the United States, April 14, 1980. Action needed to improve management and effectiveness of drug abuse treatment. U.S. General Accounting Office, HRD-80-32.

Redfield RR et al. Heterosexually acquired HTLV-III/LAV disease (AIDS related complex and AIDS), *J. Amer. Med. Assoc.* 254:2094–2096, 1985.

Robertson JR, Skidmore CA, and Roberts JJK. HIV infection in intravenous drug users: A follow-up study indicating changes in risk-taking behaviour, *Brit. J. Addict.* 83:387–391, 1988.

Scordato M. 1967–82, unbilancio dell'esperienza Svedese sulla terapia di mantenimento dei morfinodipendenti con il metadone (1967–82, an evaluation of the Swedish experience with maintenance methadone therapy of morphine addicts), *Minerva Med.* 73(47):3353–3358, 1982.

Scott NR et al. Methadone in the Southwest: A three-year follow-up of Chicano heroin addicts, *Am. J. Orthopsychiat.* 43:355–361, 1973.

Sells SB. Treatment effectiveness, in Dupont RL, Goldstein A, and O'Donnell J (eds.), *Handbook on Drug Abuse.* Washington, D.C.: U.S. Govt. Print. Off., 1979.

Sells SB and Simpson DD. *The Effectiveness of Drug Abuse Treatment* Vol. 3. Cambridge, Mass.: Ballinger, 1976.

Sells SB et al. A national follow-up study to evaluate the effectiveness of drug abuse treatment: A report on the DARP five years later, *Am J. Drug Alcohol Abuse* 4:545–556, 1976.

Senay EC. *Substance Abuse Disorders in Clinical Practice.* Littleton, Mass.: John Wright, 1983.

Senay EC et al. Withdrawal from methadone maintenance *Arch. Gen. Psychiat.* 34:361–376, 1977.

Senay EC et al. IDAP-Five year results, *Natl. Conf. Methadone Treat. Proc.* 2:1437–1464, 1973.

Senay EC and Shick JFE. Pupillography responses to methadone challenge: Aid to diagnosis of opioid dependence, *Drug and Alcohol Dependence* 3:133–138, 1978.

Shaffet A et al. Assessment of treatment outcomes in a drug abuse rehabilitation network: Newark, New Jersey, *Am. J. Drug Alcohol Abuse* 7:141, 1980.

Sheppard C et al. Indications of psychopathology in male narcotic abusers, their effects, and relation to treatment effectiveness, *J. of Psychology* 81:351–360, 1972.

Simpson DD. Treatment for drug abuse: Follow-up outcomes and length of time spent, *Arch. Gen. Psychiat.* 38:875–880, 1981.

Simpson DD, Joe GW, and Bracy SA. Six-year follow-up on

opioid addicts after admission to treatment, *Arch. Gen. Psychiatr.* 39:1318–1323, 1982.

Smialek JE et al. Methadone deaths in children: A continuing problem, *J. Amer. Med. Assoc.* 238:2516–2517, 1977.

Stimmel BR et al. The prognosis of patients detoxified from methadone maintenance: A follow-up study, *Natl. Conf. Methadone Treat. Proc.* 1:270–274, 1973.

Stimson G and Oppenheimer E. *Heroin Addiction.* London: Tavistock, 1982.

Stimson GV, Oppenheimer E, and Thorley A. Seven-year follow-up of heroin addicts: Drug use and outcome, *Brit. Med. J.* 1:1190–1192, 1978.

Strang J, Heathcote S, and Watson P. Habit-moderation in injecting drug addicts, *Health Trends* 19:16–18, 1987.

Tidone L, Goglio A, and Borra GC. AIDS in Italy (letter), *Amer. J. Drug Alcohol Abuse* 13:485–486, 1987.

Tempesta E, and Di Giannantonio M. Sharing needles and the spread of HIV in Italy's addict population, in Battjes RJ and Pickens RW (eds.), *Needle Sharing among Intravenous Drug Abusers: National and International Perspectives*, NIDA Research Monograph 80, DHHS publication number (ADM) 88-1567, 100–113, 1988.

Tuason VB and Jones WL. Methadone maintenance treatment: A report on over three years' experience, *Minn. Med.* 57:899–901, 1974.

Uchtenhagen A. Methadonbericht: Suchtmittelersatz in der Behandlung Heroinabhangiger in der Sweitz. Beilage zum Bulletin des Bundesamtes fur Gesundheitswesen. Bern, 1984.

Uchtenhagen A. Zur Behandlung Drogenabhangiger mit Methadon: Zurcherische Richtlinien und Auswertung der Therapieresultate, PRAXIS 77:351-355, 1988.

Uchtenhagen A and Zimmer-Hofler D. Heroinabhangige und ihre "normalen" Altersgenossen. Bern: Haupt, 1985.

Van Dalen PR. Ambulante detoxificatie van heroine-verslaafden, *Tijdschr Alcohol Drugs en Andere Psychotrope Stoffen* 8:216, 1982.

VanDyke HB. New analgesic drugs, *Bull. New York Acad. Sciences* 25:152-175, 1949.

Vogel VH, Isbell H, and Chapman KW. Present status of narcotic addiction, *J. Amer. Med. Assoc.* 138:1019-1026, 1948.

Waldron VD, Klint CR, and Seibel JE. Methadone overdose treated with naloxone infusion, *J. Amer. Med. Assoc.* 225:53, 1973.

Wang RIH et al. Rating the presence and severity of opiate

dependence, *Cl. Pharmacology and Therapeutics* 16:653-658, 1974.

Weber R.   Empirische Katamnese der Methadonbehandlung Opiatabhangiger bei Hausarzten im Kanton Zurich. Thesis, University of Zurich, 1983.

Weiss SH et al.   HTLV-III infection among health care workers: Association with needle-stick injuries, *J. Amer. Med. Assoc.* 254:2089-2093, 1985.

Westermeyer J.   The pro-heroin effects of anti-opium laws, *Arch. Gen. Psychiatry* 33:1135-1139, 1976.

Westermeyer J.   Medical and nonmedical treatment for narcotic addicts: A comparative study from Asia, *J. Nerv. and Ment. Dis.* 167:205-211, 1979.

Westermeyer J.   *Poppies, Pipes and People: Opium and Its Use in Laos.* Berkeley, Cal.: Univ. California Press, 1983.

Wever LJ.   Effectten van methadone-onderhoudsprogramma's (Effects of methadone maintenance programs), *Tijdschr Alcohol Drugs en Andere Psychotrope Stoffen* 11(2):86-91, 1985.

Wieland WF and Chambers CD.   Two methods of utilizing methadone in the outpatient treatment of narcotic addicts, *Int. J. Addict.* 5:431-438, 1970.

Wiepert GD, Bewley TH, and D'Orban PT.   Outcomes for 575 British opiate addicts entering treatment between 1968 and 1970, *Bull. Narc.* (Geneva) 30(1):21-32, 1978.

Wille R.   Ten-year follow-up of a representative sample of London heroin addicts: Clinic attendance, abstinence, and mortality, *Br. J. Addict.* 76/3:259-266, 1981.

Winkelstein W et al.   Sexual practices and risk of infection by the Human Immunodeficiency Virus, *J. Amer. Med. Assoc.* 257:321-352, 1987.

Woody G. Psychiatric aspects of opiate dependence: Diagnostic and therapeutic issues, in Blaine J and Julius D (eds.), *Psychodynamics of Drug Dependence,* NIDA Research Monograph 12.   Washington, D.C.: U.S. Govt. Print. Off., 1977.

Woody GE et al.   Psychotherapy for opiate addicts, *Arch. Gen. Psychiat.* 40:639-645, 1983.

World Health Organization Committee on Drugs Liable to Produce Addiction: Third Report.   WHO Technical Report 57.   Geneva: WHO, 1951.

World Health Organization.   Aids among Drug Abusers, Report on WHO Consultation, Stockholm, October 1986. Geneva: WHO, 1987.

Zimmer-Hofler D and Tschopp A. Institutionen fur Heroinabhangige aus der Sicht der Klienten, in Ladewig, D (ed.), *Drogen und Alkohol, der aktuelle Stand in der Behandlung Drogen- und Alkoholabhangiger.* Lausanne: ISPA-Press, 24-57, 1986.

Zimmer-Hofler D, Uchtenhagen A, and Fuchs W. Methadon im Prufstand. Forschungsinformationen Serie A, Nr. 8, *Sozialpsychiatrischer Dienst.* Zurich, 1987.

Index

About the Contributors

AWNI ARIF, M.D., Ph.D., is the former head of the Drug Dependence Program, Mental Health Division, World Health Organization, Geneva. Trained in medicine in Syria, he later pursued internal medicine, trained in New York, and took a doctorate in public health from Columbia. For over a decade, Dr. Arif led an international effort to establish epidemiological studies of drug dependence, treatment programs and outcome studies, and prevention projects.

JAMES COOPER, M.D., is a psychiatrist and staff member with the National Institute of Drug Abuse in Washington, D.C. He has represented the United States in numerous international meetings on drug abuse.

JAMES MADDUX, M.D., a psychiatrist, has two decades of clinical and research experience in the use of methadone for the treatment of opioid dependence. He has conducted his work in San Antonio, Texas, where Hispanic Americans compose a large proportion of his patients. He has recently retired as professor in the Department of Psychiatry, University of Texas at San Antonio.

ROBERT NEWMAN, M.D., an internist, played a major role in the establishment of methadone maintenance clinics in New York during the 1960s. He has been a pioneer in establishing legal safeguards and medical criteria for this treatment modality. He is chief of methadone clinics for New York City.

JAN ORDING, M.S.W., played a leadership role in the development of treatment services for addicted persons in Scandinavia. He has also served as a temporary staff member at the World Health Organization, on loan from the government of Sweden. He has participated in numerous international conferences on drug dependence.

JOHN PEACHEY, M.D., is a psychiatrist with the Addiction Research Foundation in Toronto, Canada. He has had extensive clinical experience in a methadone maintenance treatment program and has published clinical research on methadone maintenance.

VICHAI POSHYACHINDA, M.D., Ph.D., is an assistant professor at Chulalongkorn University and a research director at the Health Research Institute in Bangkok, Thailand, where he has directed research programs on the sociology, epidemiology, and treatment outcome of drug dependence. He has accomplished several innovative projects among the opium-producing hill tribes of northern Thailand.

EDWARD C. SENAY, M.D., is professor of psychiatry at the University of Chicago. He has had extensive experience as clinician and clinician-investigator with the use of methadone in the treatment of opioid dependence. He has consulted with addiction treatment programs in Europe and Asia.

ENRICO TEMPESTA, M.D., is a psychiatrist in Rome, Italy. He has played an active role in the establishment and evaluation of methadone maintenance in the treatment of opiate dependence.

A. H. TUMA, Ph.D., a psychologist born in Iran, participated in a controlled comparison study of methadone versus tricyclic medication in Iranian opiate addicts. After a time with the National Institute of Drug Abuse in Washington, D.C., he joined the faculty at the University of Pittsburgh as professor in the Department of Psychiatry.

AMBROSE UCHTENHAGEN, M.D., Ph.D., is professor of social psychiatry at the University of Zurich in Switzerland. He has established both abstinence-oriented and methadone-based treatment programs for opioid-dependent persons. In Europe he has been at the forefront of efforts to track the interrelationship of Acquired Immunodeficiency Syndrome (AIDS) and drug dependence.

JOSEPH WESTERMEYER, M.D., Ph.D., first undertook field study of opium dependence in Southeast Asia during the 1960s, later studying alcohol-drug abuse in the United States as well as in Asia. Between 1977 and 1990, he participated as a consultant in several WHO studies on the epidemiology assessment and treatment of drug dependence. Currently he is professor and head of Psychiatry and Behavioral Sciences at the University of Oklahoma Health Sciences Center.